AF316777

The Shepherd's Cross

The Shepherd's Cross:

The Pastoral Calling in Community Life

A. R. WEISSER

Foreword by Rick Wise

RESOURCE *Publications* • Eugene, Oregon

THE SHEPHERD'S CROSS
The Pastoral Calling in Community Life

Resource Publications
An Imprint of Wipf and Stock Publishers
199 W. 8th Ave., Suite 3
Eugene, OR 97401

www.wipfandstock.com

PAPERBACK ISBN: 979-8-3852-0106-8
HARDCOVER ISBN: 979-8-3852-0107-5
EBOOK ISBN: 979-8-3852-0108-2

VERSION NUMBER 10/23/23

To my Church on the Rock Homer family,
for showing much grace as I have grown

CONTENTS

FOUNDATIONS: PART TWO

FOREWORD

Aaron Weisser is both a friend and a pastoral neighbor, pastoring in the same small community with much the same heart and passion for the church and Christ's mission. We are different in personality and calling, yet our core passions are surprisingly similar. I have always appreciated his unwavering character and scholarly exposition of the word of God.

My first introduction to Aaron was over coffee with a mutual friend. They had a vision for a new ministry and wanted to share their excitement for the possibilities that lie ahead. Many years later our friendship has continued. What was once only a vision is now an influential ministry in our community.

There is no better teacher than experience and someone else's experience will spare us from the endless cycle of trial and error. *The Shepherd's Cross* is born out of many years of pastoral experience, lessons that can benefit Christian leaders, but particularly the pastor.

We have all used the term "cross-bearing" as though it will be useful from time to time. However, Jesus taught us that cross-bearing is daily not sporadic.

With intentionality Aaron has methodically woven cross-bearing into pastoral ministry and more broadly every Christian's life. Just as "there is no Christian life without a cross . . . there is no ministry without a cross." We must die to self and live for Christ. It is not victimization, but like Christ, a joy set before us. He continues, "I understand that God's purposes are accomplished through a cross. I understand the dying of my flesh is a prerequisite to the resurrection of my spirit." We will never truly experience the power of God in our life while fully dependent on our own talents, strengths, wisdom or self-preservation. To experience Jesus Christ is to wholeheartedly take up our cross in every situation, deny ourselves and follow him. As you turn the pages of this work you will find it spiritually challenging while encouraging and refreshing to the heart. There is hope here. Christ intended cross-bearing to meet every sinful challenge life throws at us. *The Shepherd's Cross* is an easy read but the lessons learned are eternal. You will walk away with the firm conviction that "cross-bearing is not a lesson; it is the whole ministry."[1] The author has captured the spiritual and emotional struggle of the pastor while offering hope through cross-bearing.

You will discover that your presuppositions need a thoughtful and prayerful examination, yet there is abundant practical wisdom to help pastors navigate the varied complexities of pastoral ministry. You will walk away with a fresh view of what Christ meant when He said, "take up your cross daily and follow Me." You will also be better equipped to face the practical challenges of pastoral ministry. Cross-bearing will put you on a path to an effective and rewarding pastoral ministry. A ministry in which your greatest passion is to serve Christ by faithfully shepherding his wonderful people.

Rick Wise
Senior Pastor, Glacierview Baptist Church
Homer, Alaska

---

1. See chapter 17 of this book.

PREFACE

It may prove helpful, here at the outset, to tell you a bit about my personal and author's perspective before we journey together. Most of my upbringing, church experiences, and education was nondenominational. I was not raised to embrace a particular Christian perspective or tradition. My dad came to know Christ as an adult and gave his life to ministry shortly thereafter. My parents have lived lives of noble and costly faith in action.

I have attended churches and schools that were heavy on free choice and heavy on the Holy Spirit's role in the life of the believer. And I have attended churches and schools that were heavy on God's sovereignty and heavy on careful exegesis of Scripture. Some of my theological and ecclesiological influences have been Wayne Grudem, D. A. Carson, John Piper, Tim Keller, and Nancy Pearcey. I love and revere the word of God and operate with a high expectation for the Holy Spirit's day-to-day work in the life of the believer.

I believe the Bible is the inerrant word of God and yet observe that for all of human history we have been asking the question "Did God really say . . . ?"[2] I believe the Scriptures present the good news of God's great love for humanity, the bad news of our fallen state, and the means by which we are restored into relationship with him. I believe that Christ is returning for his church and that I have been invited to play a role in the beautification and preparation of his bride.

I planted our church along with a friend of mine in 2008. As a church plant, we initially received a small amount of financial

2. Gen 3:1.

support from a nondenominational sending church. From the beginning, it was up to us to figure out how to make things work as an independent organization. We are an unaffiliated elder-led church and I function as one of the elders. I lead our staff and ministry programs with input and support from our church elders. We have a separate board of directors tasked with governing matters of ethics and prudence on behalf of the corporation. We serve in a high-trust, high-accountability environment. I have a lot of latitude to make critical decisions about personnel and programs, but I answer to my elders and board.

We use a simple church ministry model with a focus on equipping and encouraging disciple-makers who love God and others. Because we are a fishing community, we do not offer recurring ministry programs other than our Sunday morning service during the summer months. We experience a seismic shift in our population during those months with seasonal workers leaving and seasonal residents returning. Rather than fight against these annual changes, we have embraced them and worked them in our favor.

Our community has a strong family and work ethic. Our church includes many multigenerational families. It has been an amazing place to raise our eight children. In our context, faith cannot be easily sequestered into a private compartment. We are all connected by work and money and politics and family and schools and sports and everything in between. If my faith isn't transforming me into the image of Christ, everyone is going to find out eventually. I like that about here.

If you ever want to visit one of the most beautiful places in the world, come and pay us a visit. The mountains, glaciers, and beaches will take your breath away. God lives here.

As you read, I pray you will begin to think in new ways about the ministry of shepherding. Second, I hope that this new way of thinking coincides with a continued transformation of your heart, ultimately impacting your capacity to engage the people you shepherd, with joy. Toward this end, there are two primary portions of the book: Foundations and Practicum.

The Foundation portions provide the theological and philosophical groundwork for understanding the nature of cross-bearing. I then expand that foundation to encompass theologically laden and familiar terms like love, righteousness, and justice. My goal here is a more integrated thought process. However, the Foundations section is a bit of a heavy lift so I opted to split it into two parts.

The Practicum portions are where I work through real and common examples of cross-bearing as it plays out both in the heart of the shepherd and in shepherding relationships. The Practicum portions put flesh to the ideas presented in parts one and two of Foundations and draw heavily from my own experiences. Much of it will sound familiar!

The Examen section should be read and reread as you evaluate your own life and calling as a shepherd. Am I really called? Can I sustain this calling? Can I finish well? These are questions to be approached with prayer.

And finally, I included a few additional thoughts in the Addendum that just did not fit well anywhere else and yet seemed important to mention.

Enjoy.

FOUNDATIONS
Part One

INTRODUCTION: SURPRISE

THE UNEXPECTEDNESS OF EVERYTHING

On a late fall day many years ago, I pulled in to visit our local grocer and while there, decided a latte from Starbucks was in order. As I stood at the register waiting for the barista to take my order I noticed a young man standing about twenty feet behind me, a little to my left.

Although I am naturally a quiet observer of others, content to avoid direct engagement, I had grown in my capacity to initiate friendly interactions when out and about in my home town. I recognized this young man as a recent addition to our church. I am the pastor and planter of a small nondenominational congregation that meets at the local high school. He had attended the previous three or four weeks of Sunday morning services but sat in the back corner of the bleachers and was quick to leave as worship came to a close.

After ordering my grande nonfat latte with whipped cream, I approached him to introduce myself and say hello. Medium height and build, long, dark hair pulled into a low knot, he wore John Lennon spectacles and was otherwise simply dressed. His demeanor was unassuming. As I reached out my hand to say hello he looked up and began to sharply cuss me out. Because he didn't offer any context or explanation, I thought it best to turn around, grab my coffee and head out the door.

Once I had reached my truck I paused for a moment. I wondered if I had somehow offended him without knowing it and should take responsibility to repair the inadvertent harm. With an elevated heart rate, I walked back into the store and found him standing in the same place looking at his phone. I approached him again, this time more cautiously, and offered, "It seems that you are upset at me but I don't know why. Did I say or do something to offend you?"

Maybe I should have just hopped in my truck and left after the first interaction. If he wanted me to know his anger the first time, now he wanted the rest of the customers to know it. He re-launched his profane tirade but this time with the volume cranked up several notches. I was starting to feel a little embarrassed. Then he asked me to get away from him. I left, very confused.

The following Sunday as I opened our service with a welcome, I was surprised to see the same young man sitting in the back corner seat he had occupied the weeks prior. When the service closed, he approached me. I was a little on edge. To my surprise, he apologized. He went on to acknowledge that he was angry about a particular position that I had expressed on the subject of human sexuality. When I asked him to tell me more, he declined.

I never saw him again.

The church that I lead is in the small, rural town of Homer, Alaska. As the grandson of Alaskan homesteaders, this is the place of my birth and my heritage. When I was ten my family moved overseas to the city of Manila, called by God to serve the blind and visually impaired population. It was there that I met my future wife, the daughter of church planters and translators ministering to the unreached. My years overseas threw my life in Alaska into sharp relief. I carry a deep sense of this place being my home and yet have always carried a subtle sense of being an outsider.

The history of Homer's faith community is complex. The last half century is interspersed with periods of great growth and periods of seismic struggle. There are several small churches with their various identities and faith expressions. And yet Sunday morning is the only time we are separated. Christians in our small town seem bonded regardless of where we worship. We work together, play together, raise our kids together, and come together to mourn the dead.

It was here that I first heard my calling and here that I have lived it out. I am called to shepherd. Shepherding as a framework for understanding pastoral ministry fits well with my rural lifestyle. Jesus is our shepherd[1] and I his under-shepherd.[2] He calls me to kindly care for his flock, to lead his flock to reliable sustenance and to protect them from threats. Many shepherds do not carry the formal title of pastor, priest, or reverend. But a pastor-shepherd is one uniquely called to provide spiritual care for God's people. If you are taking your first steps on this journey, you have much to look forward to.

The call to vocational ministry is exhilarating for those who receive it. It was for me, in the most terrifying and wonderful way. The possibilities and potential seemed endlessly before me, further than the eye could see or the mind imagine. Some would cheer me on, some would prophetically assure me of success, some would come alongside me and pledge their support. Moving into ministry felt like coming alive.

If you are one of the called, you know this joy and wonderment. Even if you resist at first, getting in step with God's calling is a rush.

I remember well the first time I opened the word of God with an audience of adults, my church. Despite my overpowering nervousness I felt a sense of rightness in the role. Consistent with my young age and immaturity, what I lacked in expertise and experience, I made up for with enthusiasm. And people responded. They saw past my youthful clunkiness and encouraged my gift.

There was so much grace in those first years. The people who knew me wanted to see me succeed.

1. John 10:11: "I am the good shepherd. The good shepherd lays down his life for the sheep."

2. 1 Pet 5:1–4: "Therefore, I urge elders among you, as your fellow elder and a witness of the sufferings of Christ, and one who is also a fellow partaker of the glory that is to be revealed: shepherd the flock of God among you, exercising oversight, not under compulsion but voluntarily, according to the will of God; and not with greed but with eagerness; nor yet as domineering over those assigned to your care, but by proving to be examples to the flock. And when the Chief Shepherd appears, you will receive the unfading crown of glory."

Pastoral ministry has been one of the greatest joys of my life. But joy did not come in the way I expected. There is a joy in ministry that is much greater than I expected, and I came within inches of missing that joy entirely. Like a ship passing the tip of a great continent in the dead of night, this joy is vast, unexpected, and easy to miss. There are shepherds who will never know this joy.

The initial rush of excitement in ministry will fade. It must. Much of the early reward of ministry done well was rooted in the building up of my own ego, the gratification of the "natural man."[3] I did not glory in my weakness but rather in my strength[4]—giving God the credit for my strength, of course.

The well-meaning encouragement of others in those early years served to feed the dying flesh. But all flesh, and all of its appetites, must die.[5] It is only ministry understood as an opportunity to die that reduces my temptation to eventually hate it. It is only when I walk in the power of a crucified life that my ministry will be anything more than powerless. It is only when I have fallen to the ground and perished that will I bear much fruit.[6] If I save anything for the fallen self that thing will cost me all of it.

I am writing because I want to help you discover this true joy. And to remind myself again where this true joy is found. It is an elusive, unexpected prize.

If you are called to pastoral ministry, I want to invite you to take up your shepherd's cross. There is great joy set before us.

Let's journey together.

---

3. 1 Cor 2:14: "But a natural person does not accept the things of the Spirit of God, for they are foolishness to him; and he cannot understand them, because they are spiritually discerned."

4. 2 Cor 12:9: "And He has said to me, 'My grace is sufficient for you, for power is perfected in weakness.' Most gladly, therefore, I will rather boast about my weaknesses, so that the power of Christ may dwell in me."

5. Rom 8:13: "For if you are living in accord with the flesh, you are going to die; but if by the Spirit you are putting to death the deeds of the body, you will live."

6. John 12:24: "Truly, truly I say to you, unless a grain of wheat falls into the earth and dies, it remains alone; but if it dies, it bears much fruit."

Chapter 1

THE CROSS

THE FOUNDATION OF GOD'S INTENTIONS

God hold us to that which drew us first, when the Cross
was the attraction, and we wanted nothing else.

AMY CARMICHAEL

In the final moments, at the last temptation, Jesus prayed to his
Father, alone in the garden. "If it is possible, take this cup from
me."[1]

God, if there is a plan B, if there is another option, if there is
an exit ramp, please show it to me now. What we don't hear is the
other side of the conversation.

There was no plan B. There was no other option. There was
no exit ramp. If Jesus was to accomplish the Father's will, there
was only plan A. He must be mocked, beaten, crucified, and killed.
That was plan A.

The execution of this plan was evil at its finest. The executors
were both evil in their hostility and evil in their indifference. There
had never been and would never be again such a grave miscarriage
of justice. The anguish of betrayal would be mixed with the pain

1. Luke 22:42.

of desertion and the agony of a brutal death by torture. That was plan A.

Those who knew him would look and say "innocence died today." And that was true. But from the vantage point of heaven his death meant something else. Evil died that day. Sin died that day. Humanity's great nemesis, death died that day.[2] And evil and sin and death were crushed for all of eternity in the physical body of Jesus.[3] "What you intended for evil, God intended for good."[4] That was plan A.

If we say that our God is omniscient and omnipotent, there was only ever plan A. There never was, in all of eternity, any plan other than the cross. God would create humankind, we would reject his love, and his love would be expressed for us in this way; while we were still sinners, he died for us. The cross is not only central to our understanding of salvation, it is bedrock to our comprehension of God's love.

The cross is the inextricable core of the supreme ethic of Christianity; love God and love your neighbor. It is not a piece, a facet, a component of Christian love. God demonstrates his love by dying on a cross.[5] If you want to know what divine love looks like in the context of sinful humanity, you have one picture for your reference, a cross.

There is a good chance you chose to minister because you love people. You love helping people. There is also a good chance you didn't expect the price of love to be so high. The shooting pain of that first hammer swing as the spikes pierce flesh and bone is shocking. You likely consoled yourself with quiet reassurances. "There's been a misunderstanding and surely we will work this out." Your reassurances did not look like a cross.

2. 2 Tim 1:10b: "Our Savior Christ Jesus, who abolished death and brought life and immortality to light through the gospel."

3. 1 Pet 2:24: "And He Himself brought our sins in His body up on the cross, so that we might die to sin and live for righteousness; by His wounds you were healed."

4. Gen 50:20.

5. Rom 5:8: "But God demonstrates His own love toward us, in that while we were still sinners, Christ died for us."

When our reassurances look like something other than a cross, we are positioned to miss the point. We become disillusioned. We grow bitter. We recoil not just because the pain is unbearable, but because it is so unexpected. And for many who are committed to sticking it out, it is in these moments we abandon God's plan A and pour our hearts and souls into figuring out a plan B: a cross-less ministry.

But there is no ministry without a cross. We should have known that. Jesus warned us there is no Christian life without a cross. There is no following Jesus without a cross. As ministers we are called to show others this cross calling, not disintegrate in fear when it comes upon us. This is Spiritual Maturity 101: "if anyone would come after me, he must deny himself, take up his cross, and follow me."[6]

You cannot call others to die when you refuse even to lie still. You cannot demonstrate the love of God and refuse the cross. You cannot walk in the power of his resurrection if you have not united yourself with his death.[7]

But why? Why would anyone sign up for this? Even more pressing, why did *he* sign up for this? He, unlike us, had the opportunity to cancel or change the plan. Why did an omnipotent, omniscient, eternal God choose a plan A that involved the agony of a cross? For the joy set before him.[8] The omnipotent, omniscient, eternal God chose a cross because it was the pathway to a greater joy than would have been available on any alternate path.

The ministry ambitions of Jesus were not much different from your own. Jesus wanted a small group of leader followers who would embrace and advance the kingdom of God. Jesus wanted crowds to turn to God. Jesus wanted religious and political leaders to find repentance. So he laid his life down. He took up his cross.

6. Matt 16:24.

7. Phil 3:10: "That I may know Him and the power of His resurrection and the fellowship of His sufferings, being conformed to His death."

8. Heb 12:2: "Looking only at Jesus, the originator and perfecter of the faith, who for the joy set before Him endured the cross, despising the shame, and has sat down at the right hand of the throne of God."

This strategy for the advancement of Christ's purpose was so counterintuitive to his disciples, they not only rejected it outright, they rebuked him for suggesting it.[9] Any alternative to the accumulation of social, political, and religious clout was a strategy not worth considering. The idea of success through tortured death? Ludicrous. And yet it was their unwillingness to come to terms with God's plan that made them unable to offer their strong support and much needed comfort. "Could you not stay awake for even a short while?"[10]

Peter brandished a sword when prayer was required. Overflowing with moral conviction, Peter was ready to bring the fight and shut down plan A. He could not, would not, come to terms with what was unfolding in front of his own eyes. Surely there has been a great misunderstanding! Surely, we can work this out. Peter's internal reassurances did not include a cross.

The cross is a call not just for shepherds. It is Christ's call to the sheep. "If anyone would come after me, he must." Anyone. Everyone. But how will any pastor effectively lead if the fervent prayer of "Take this cup from me" never becomes the resolute prayer of "Not my will, but yours"?

The shepherd is not tasked merely with developing the internal strength to refrain from brandishing a weapon. He is to lead by instructing others to lay down their swords on his behalf. He is to lead by reminding his sheep that the God of the universe has legions of angels standing at the ready.

He does not ask for pity. "Weep not for me."[11] He leads through the calm resolve of taking up the cross and wrestling it onto his own two shoulders in joyful obedience to the resurrected Christ.

As a young pastor I would have been fine with this. Sure, no problem. I'll take up my cross. I get it; ministry can be hard. Moving right along.

---

9. Matt 16:22: "And yet Peter took Him aside and began to rebuke Him, saying, 'God forbid it, Lord! This shall never happen to You!'"

10. Matt 26:40.

11. Luke 23:28.

What I didn't expect was that carrying a cross felt so much like dying. Dying is awful. It is brutal. There is nothing worse. And the carnal man does not go down easy. There are swords lying everywhere within reach just begging to be brandished. "This could all stop" they whisper. "You don't deserve this."

But even in death we find God's grace. It is the promise that sin has an expiration date. It is the full and final defeat of pain, sorrow, and evil. "He must not eat of the tree of life and live forever with the knowledge of good and evil."[12] God's promise to crush sin is fulfilled through death. His promise to defeat death is fulfilled through resurrection. But there is no resurrection until there is a death. Death is its prerequisite.

Do you want your ministry to ooze with resurrection power? Take up your cross. The sooner your ego, your expectations, your insecurities, your fears, your visions and aspirations all die, the sooner you can walk in resurrection life. Yes, vision is necessary. But even a little bit of the flesh is a little bit too much. So wrestle that wooden beam on your shoulders and start walking.

Set your eyes on Golgotha. Embrace the agony of plan A for the joy before you.

And prepare to meet the team; accusers, betrayers, and crucifiers, some of whom may be your friends.

12. Gen 3:22.

Chapter 2

THE CRUCIFIER

A HEART FOR THOSE WHO DO HARM

A crucifixion is no natural disaster. It is not death by drowning. It is not death by lightning bolt. It is murder. It is one person acting against another.

When Jesus said "Unless you drink my blood, you have no life in yourselves"[1] he calls out generations of Jewish blood veneration. Blood had forever been indicative of the life of a creature all the way from Gen 9 and discussed in detail in Lev 17.

But blood becomes indicative of the life of a creature only in death. More specifically, death by violence. It is blood *poured out* that is representative of the life of the creature.

A crucifixion is a bloodletting. It is a murder, whether legal or not. A cross is a manmade instrument of violent death. The lifeblood of the Eucharist is the blood poured out through death by crucifixion.

This is not a blood bank with its sterile instruments and careful extractions. There are no small vials of exactly the right amount so as not to make the donor week and faint.

The blood of Jesus is made available only through his violent, government-sanctioned homicide. "This is my blood, poured

---

1. John 6:53.

out."[2] This is the blood offered to us. This is the blood without which we have no life in and of ourselves. It is the lifeblood of Jesus, made to flow by evil, and given as a gift.

And Jesus went willingly, in obedience to the Father's plan A. He went to the cross, and gave his life, his blood. Blood made to flow through many lashings, nails piercing flesh, and a spear in his side. Blood poured out.

For whom exactly?

For those who extracted it. For the crucifiers.

To properly understand the ministry of cross-bearing, we must accept that the crucifixion of Jesus was in service to the crucifiers. His blood was poured out in service to those who violently made it flow.

"Father, forgive them, for they know not what they do."[3]

He did not pray "Father, stop them, for they know not what they do." No. They, of all people, will have no hope apart from the hope that is now made available by their evil deed. To pray "Father, forgive them" is to ask that God would make the cleansing benefits of the cross available to the very men who were pounding the nails.

To pray "Father, forgive them" is to ask that the bloodletters would gain access to the life-blood of their victim. It is to pray that the perpetrators would become the beneficiaries. Because unless you drink his blood, you have no life in and of yourselves. Place your cup under the wound that you have opened up.

It is an easy thing to casually drop the phrase "my cross to bear" in the context of Christian life and ministry. I do this often in the context of minor slights where I chose to be the bigger man.

A church member expresses disappointment in her small group experience and blames the ministry model I enacted. But I am respectful in my reply. I guess this is my cross to bear.

A neighbor's tree falls on my backyard shed. It took me $200 and three hours of my Saturday to repair it. But I am cheerful. I guess this is my cross to bear.

2. Matt 26:28.

3. Luke 23:34.

My vehicle is in need of unexpected and expensive repairs. But I do not complain. I guess this is my cross to bear.

Don't get me wrong. I do not in anyway want to diminish the value of patience, kindness, and joy in the face of everyday challenges. Our hearts are both revealed and formed through these mundane experiences. But if you actually believe that these experiences are the heart of cross-bearing, you are about to get steamrolled.

Crosses require crucifiers.

One of Jesus's closest friends sold directions to his whereabouts to a group of murderous thugs for a month's wages.[4] Ouch.

When the rest of his close friends realized that he wasn't going to make his own innocence his cause, they deserted him.[5]

Except Peter. Peter, true to his promise, was ready to go the distance. He brandished his sword and despite being outnumbered and outgunned by the Roman cohort, he was ready to rumble.[6] Peter was ready to die in defiance of his crucifiers. Peter was not ready to die in service of his crucifiers. Not yet.

The vast and surprising expanse of joy that is "set before me" in ministry is the joy found on the other side of taking up my cross in service of the crucifiers. It is on the other side of the excruciating all-out war against the flesh that unfolds in the garden of Gethsemane. "Father, if there is a plan B, now is the time." "Father, if you are willing, take this cup from me." But finally, resolutely, and unequivocally "not my will, but Yours be done."

It is when confronted with the crucifixion of my ego at the hands of the very people I have committed my life to serve, that I learn my true calling. Because what they intend for evil, God intends for good, to usher me into a greater experience of the resurrected life of Jesus. After all, it is the survival of my flesh with all of its insatiable yet broken appetites that represents the greatest threat to my experience of the abiding life of God. Why would

---

4. Matt 26:14-15.

5. Matt 26:56.

6. John 18:10.

I resent the person who drives in the death nail? Is he not God's instrument?

"Father, forgive them, they know not what they do."

They ushered him through the doorway of death, the final test, to the joy set before him. Through his stripes, they are healed.[7] "They know not what they do." But he knew. He came for this purpose.

The crucifixion of Jesus was in service of the crucifiers.

To shepherd the flock of God through the ministry of the cross is to grow in the supernatural capacity to love those who do you harm. It is to look with compassion into the eyes of the one wielding the hammer and to *want* forgiveness for that person. This supernatural love is so pure and so unshakeable it is not weakened as the hammer blows rain down. It is instead awakened, enlivened, and enlarged by the assault against its existence.

There is an alarming and defining moment that most, if not all, shepherds encounter; the moment when you realize your friend is your betrayer. The moment when the person who believed in you, supported you, and encouraged you, stops doing so. Unlike Judas, they probably didn't sell your life for a month's wage. But very much like Judas, they have developed a distaste for your ministry decisions and priorities.[8]

I remember the first time a formerly vocal cheerleader informed me that I had fallen from favor and was therefore expendable. In this person's eyes, I was now an obstacle. In that moment all of the previous flatteries suddenly felt as if they had been given on loan and were now being collected with interest. In place of my inflated sense of pride was a hollow and hungry gut. The same appetite that was enlarged by the satiating effect of positive encouragement writhed in pain when those niceties were discontinued.

In your case, maybe it was an elder or a board member. Maybe a senior pastor. Maybe it was a subordinate. You remember that shuddering realization; this person is not on my team. You remember the shock of discovering that this friend of yours was

7. Isa 53:5.
8. John 12:4–6.

acting against you. You laid down your life as a sacrifice in obedience to the call of God. And they want you gone. They want you out. You are the problem, and they are the solution.

Maybe they malign you or undermine you. Maybe they work to turn other friends against you. Maybe they outright refuse to cooperate and busy themselves creating barriers to your leadership and influence. Or maybe they get punitive and seek to do harm to your finances and your future opportunities. The strategies are as creative as they are many.

But do not be distracted. This is not about them. This is about you. This is your invitation to embrace the crucified life. This is your invitation to lay your life down for the joy set before you. Now you must decide if you, as the shepherd, will lead by example in taking up your cross.

Everything you preach and everything you believe about the gospel is brought to bear in your response to the one who takes the 30 shekels, who drives the nails, who thrusts the spear. For the one who has embraced ministry as an opportunity to die, the dying feels hopeful. It is purposeful. I do not deny the pain of it or the sin of it. But I understand that God's purposes are accomplished through a cross. I understand the dying of my flesh is the prerequisite to the resurrection of my Spirit.

The fellowship of sharing in the sufferings of Jesus becomes a sweet source of unshakeable joy that opens up into a life of peace.

The ministry of the cross is a ministry of laser focus. It is a ministry of love at all cost. It is realized in the heart of the shepherd who wants the crucifier to know God's forgiveness more than he wants the pain to stop. No languishing self-pity. Only loving self-sacrifice. Cross-bearers are willing to sustain the pain in hopes that the crucifier might find freedom and forgiveness.

Of course, there is an alternative.

Disappointment and resentment that grows into bitterness and cutting cynicism. The final outcome is an embittered tired shepherd. "Watch out," they warn. "Those sheep are not who you think they are. You need to protect yourself! Don't get too close or you will get burned." They believe their experiences have produced practical wisdom that I need to hear.

What they are really warning me about is the cross with its crucifiers. Ministry could have been great. Except for the few who ruined it. Except for those few who obliterated my ego and self-confidence. Betrayers. Deserters. Crucifiers. They took my joy, stole it by force.

This is all a lie that our flesh heartily agrees with.

Remember, the cross was God's plan A from the foundation of the world. The cross is not the backup plan. The cross is not settling for less. The cross is the only pathway to God's greatest joy. If there was another way, the Father would have granted it. To Jesus. And to you.

Chapter 3

TIMING

PROACTIVE SUBMISSION AND ESCAPE

Once I have unequivocally embraced the invitation to take up my cross and follow in the footsteps of Jesus, I am ready. Now to pick a date.

Truth be told, there will be more invitations to be crucified than you are reasonably able to accept. After all, your calendar will require other obligations and duties as well. Some days and weeks are not ideal for dying, but this is a decision only the mature are prepared to make.

When Jesus was still an infant, Herod would have gladly placed him on the cross. He was prepared to end this king's reign before it began. But it wasn't a good time. So the angel told Joseph to get out of town for a while. Better get away to Egypt and wait this one out.[1]

In Luke 4 a small and angry crowd escorted Jesus to a cliff. They were ready to bring his popular ministry to a sudden end. A cliff, a cross—the goal is the same. But it wasn't a good time. So Jesus sneaked out of there. There were other obligations and duties to tend to.

In John 7 and 8 several crowds sought to do him in. One group gathered stones to put Jesus to death by projectile. It was

---

1. Matt 2.

time to deal with this man once and for all. But it wasn't a good time. So Jesus escaped. He got away. There were other obligations and duties to tend to.

Later on, when the group of gangsters showed up in Gethsemane, Peter sprung to action. And it was a good time. It was the right time. So Jesus went with them and died. There were no other obligations or duties to tend to.

When his life and ministry were threatened, Jesus chose between two options: get away or go along. Much to Peter's initial dismay, there was no third "fight back in God's name" option. Eventually, all of Jesus's disciples accepted this construct. As did Paul. Paul's ministry was characterized by many *getaway* moments.[2] Then he made a deliberate decision to *go along*. And it cost him his life.

Paul knew that going along might cost him his life. He went along any way.[3] And how did Paul know it was time to stop getting away and time to go along? God's Spirit had revealed it to him. It is the only way any shepherd knows when it is time to get away or time to go along. God must reveal it and the shepherd must discern it.

Almost all discussion of the crucified life in the context of ministry brings to the surface a shared fear that is often expressed. It is a fear that is illustrated by a common household item. "I am not going to be a doormat." To be a doormat is to be walked all over or trampled on.

There will come a time in your ministry when someone will stand against you. They will pose a real threat to your continuation. They will have the capacity to do harm to your ministry. But you don't have to be a doormat. Jesus was not a doormat. Jesus has provided you with two proactive options; get away or go along. Both are purposeful, both are motivated by obedience.

How do you know when it is time to get away or go along? I have used and heard a few common criteria for discernment in discussions about ministry and suffering. These indicators help me

2. Acts 9:23–25; 13:50; 14:6; 17:10.
3. Acts 21:13.

know when it is time to die. These criteria are convenient in that they soundly rule out most opportunities to take up a cross and explain that avoidance with sound logic and godly motivation.

I will only do what brings me joy. There is some wisdom in this general orientation. You should do that which will bring you maximum joy in Jesus. But this criterion is misleading if understood within a narrowly sensory context. A trite version of this is "If you're not having fun, why do it?" If I believe the pathway to maximum joy will always feel joyful as I walk on it, I will be easily persuaded to veer off this path. Maximum joy is resurrection life. It lies just on the other side of death and crucifixion. Taking up your cross will not feel joyful, but it will lead you to joy. To find your life, you must lose it.[4]

I will never enable bad behavior. This criterion assumes that any bad behavior I encounter is my bad behavior to fix. To do otherwise is to enable sin and to make myself culpable for the sin of others by allowing it. The only problem with this logic is that if Jesus had applied it, he would never have submitted to the cross. Subordinates use this explanation to defend their insubordination. But it is possible for righteous indignation to be a disguise for self-righteousness. "If they force you to go a mile, go two miles."[5] Jesus enabled a lot of bad behavior.

I will always fight for justice. And you should. But you should also understand that God accomplishes his justice in his timeframe by his methods.[6] Jesus submitted to injustice and determined not to make his own innocence his cause. When reviled, he did not revile.[7] He never once doubted that the Father would ensure that justice was served. But he also knew that mercy triumphs over

---

4. Matt 10:39: "The one who has found his life will lose it, and the one who has lost his life on My account will find it."

5. Matt 5:41.

6. 2 Pet 3:3–9.

7. 1 Pet 2:23: "And while being abusively insulted, He did not insult in return; while suffering, He did not threaten, but kept entrusting Himself to Him who judges righteously."

judgment.[8] Sometimes leaders are called to deny themselves, take up their cross and give room for the justice of God. Sometimes what others intend for evil God *intends* for good.

I will do what pleases others. This leader assumes that every antagonism should be embraced as an opportunity to die. This leader never attempts to get away, but always and only goes along. As a result, he is unfocused and unable to follow through toward long term goals. Other people are allowed to dictate priorities and schedules. Because to say yes to everyone is to abandon redemptive cross-carrying and, in fact, become a doormat. Remember, getting away is a legitimate option that Jesus chose many times.

If it hurts it must be spiritual. This is the most pious option. And the difficulty of facing painful things head-on can become a distorted version of religiosity. Undoubtedly this is a courageous option. But doing the hard thing is not always the same as doing the God-honoring thing. And very quickly, always doing the hard thing can become a source of self-righteous pride. Sometimes getting away is the best way to serve others and obey God. Sometimes getting away is the most redemptive option.

But whether you get away or go along, you are always fully in the driver's seat. These need to be careful and premeditated decisions. The choice requires thoughtful deliberation and a keen ear for the Holy Spirit. Cross-bearers are never just along for the ride. Cross-bearers are never victims of circumstance. "Do you not know I could appeal to the Father for the immediate dispatch of over 72,000 angels?"[9] Jesus went along in obedience to his Father's will.

If anyone would be my disciple, he must deny himself, take up his cross, and follow me. Self-denial is the most fundamental prerequisite for cross-bearers. As a cross-bearer, I have learned to remove natural will and my immediate interests from the equation. My guiding question is not "What will this cost me?" My guiding question is "Which way is God leading?" Because wherever God

8. Jas 2:13: "For judgment will be merciless to one who has shown no mercy; mercy triumphs over judgment."

9. Matt 26:53.

leads is the pathway to the greatest experience of joy and peace that is available.

Self-denial.

Cross-bearing.

Only then can you follow.

And once you have committed to this path, Satan is going to show up. But probably not in the form you might expect.

Chapter 4

SATAN

REFUSING WELL-INTENTIONED RESCUERS

Many of the sermons I have heard on the life of Peter have included chiding critiques. Peter made some big mistakes. He was passionate and impulsive, often totally clueless to the will of God, locked into the sociopolitical construct of his upbringing. He was sometimes so ambitiously off course his scenes almost read as comedy in the Gospels. Yet Peter is the kind of guy you want as a close friend. He was loyal and self-sacrificing to a fault, even when seemingly out of touch with the present moment.

It was shortly after Peter made his famous confession of Jesus the Christ, the Messiah, that Jesus began to explain to his boys what was about to go down. First, he was going to go to Jerusalem because he must. Then, once there, the religious leaders who despised him would persecute him intensely. Eventually, they would kill him. But after being killed, Jesus planned to return three days later.

Peter wasn't having it. But Peter was a good friend, so he wanted to handle this looming threat with some tact. He pulled Jesus aside, so as not to embarrass him in front of their friends. After getting him alone, Peter rebuked Jesus for his public predictions of pending doom. And his rebuke was not hollow. "God forbid it!

Lord, this shall never happen to You."[1] It was not just Peter who was unwilling to let such a tragedy occur; God would not allow it. Or so Peter believed.

Everyone needs a Peter. He is so validating to our natural instincts. Peter provides one of the most needed gifts ever offered to a sufferer, protection. He had come to the conclusion that Jesus was the promised Messiah, the fulfillment of prophecy and the long-awaited deliverer promised to the nation. As such, Jesus certainly would not submit to the jealous persecution of a pack of religious imposters and posers. Absolutely not.

Peter was the friend who would have Jesus's back. He would go to bat if necessary and risk his own safety. Why such confidence? Because Jesus was his friend, and because God was on Peter's side against the evil forces who would do harm.

Not only did Peter offer his protection, he validated Jesus's importance. In the very next chapter he offered to build a tabernacle for Jesus, a place to establish the throne he was entitled to as King![2] Peter's stern rebuke to Jesus was in part in recognition of the status that Jesus truly deserved. Someone else might go and endure persecution and even murder, but not Jesus. Jesus was far too important, too critical to the storyline to get knocked out. You don't kill off the star of the show, you kill off the no-name extra, or better yet, the villain.

What Peter did not realize is that his protective instincts aligned him with Satan, the enemy of God, the accuser of the brethren, the father of lies. Peter loved Jesus with the selfish love of someone deeply in need. "Jesus, I need you to stick around, so stop talking about dying!" Peter did not know how to love with the unselfish love of letting someone serve God's purposes no matter the cost. I think Peter's words and actions prove that he would rather have died himself than to stand by while Jesus was killed.

We all need the fierce love of a Peter in our lives. But best friends can easily align with Satan while claiming alignment with

1. Matt 16:22.
2. Matt 17:4.

God in your defense. "God forbid it!" They will not stand by and allow you to be harmed. How could a good friend be so callous?

"Get behind me Satan! You are a stumbling block to Me; for you are not setting your mind on God's interests but man's."[3] I believe the hardest part of having great friends who are aligned with Jesus is standing back and allowing them to walk through suffering without lifting a finger to rescue them. It doesn't feel like friendship. I am so thankful for the protective tendencies of those who care about me. It feels good!

But our best friends cannot be allowed to stand in the way of cross-bearing. And it doesn't matter their motive. If God has called me to carry this cross, you must allow it. If God has called my loved one to carry a cross, I must allow it.

Still, there is a final temptation, a parting gift I desire from those that would ensure my protection and validate my sense of importance. If you cannot get in the way, if you cannot stop what is about to happen, if this is what God wills; as a mere token of your affection, could you at least extend to me your pity? That is the only gift my natural self requires.

This was a gift Jesus flatly rejected. "And following Him was a large crowd of people, and of women who were mourning and lamenting Him. But Jesus, turning to them, said, "Daughters of Jerusalem, stop weeping for me.'"[4]

Encouragement? Sure. Gratitude? Of course. Pity? An emphatic no. Jesus scorned the shame of it. Why would the Son of God need to be pitied for the path that he had chosen for himself? The cross of Luke 23 was no different than the creation story of Gen 1. The eternally begotten Son of God in union with the triune Godhead had willed it, had desired it, and so did it! Do not weep for me! I am here by my will, by my choice, for the joy set before me.

For some wounded soldiers, pity is the only morphine available. As I languish in the agony of my treacherous treatment, my sense of victimization consoles my own heart. To receive pity

---

3. Matt 16:23.

4. Luke 23:27–28.

from others is to allow them to affirm my victim status. Unhealthy codependent relationships easily take root in the fertile soil of the injured soul in search of commiseration.

Cross-bearers decline protection: "I won't let this happen to you."

Cross-bearers decline assertions of their own prominence: "This is beneath you."

Cross-bearers decline pity: "You poor thing, you don't deserve this."

No wonder the disciples fled. What other options were they offered?

And having declined all three, I find myself in unchartered waters. The normal moorings that would have offered some consolation through the storm are no longer available, leaving me feeling lost and profoundly alone. The manner in which I have grown accustomed to drawing strength from others is now off limits. What then?

How am I to enter into the dark waters of vulnerability when my coping mechanisms for managing my feelings of vulnerability have been removed? What are good friends for if not to validate me?

But it is here, after losing my grip on my feeble stabilizers, that I discover one of the greatest surprises of all.

And my greatest strength.

Chapter 5

FELLOWSHIP

THE MOST BEAUTIFUL GIFT

Cross-bearing has a way of revealing my subconscious values. Of course, any good shepherd will claim to be motivated by noble aspirations. I'm after whatever it is that a pastor should be after; God's glory, kingdom advancement, disciples, a healthy church, etc, etc. And many of us are sincere.

I came into ministry with a fairly stable and healthy relationship with God. I was growing in freedom and confidence in God's calling upon my life. And if you had asked me what my ministry intentions were, I would have given a satisfactory answer. No red flags.

If you had loaded the question, rather than leaving it open-ended, and asked "Is it your greatest aspiration in ministry to experience a greater degree of fellowship with Jesus?" I would have answered that correctly as well. Yes, of course.

Most living, breathing ministry candidates will get that answer right. We go into the shepherding ministry wanting greater fellowship with the triumphal, resurrected King Jesus. Who wouldn't want the support of the greatest power in the universe to assist in accomplishing such noble goals?! Have you read Revelation 1? Yes, I want to make sure that guy is on my team.

But there is an order to things. Christ walked it out for us. Paul spelled it out for us, "that I may know the power of His resurrection and the fellowship of His sufferings, being conformed to His death."[1] The power of resurrection is the product of the crucifixion.

And here comes the surprise. Cross-bearing is the pathway to the deepest fellowship with Jesus that can be experienced this side of heaven. If it is close contact with Jesus that I desire, it is found in serving others by bearing up under suffering that I do not deserve. It was the hardest thing Jesus ever did.

And it is there, at the end of my rope, at the outer limits of where my will can take me, that I find the refreshing flood of comfort in Christ's immanence. Jesus walked that road alone and in his great mercy, never requires the same from us. "For just as the sufferings of Christ are ours in abundance, so also our comfort is abundant through Christ."[2]

"For since He Himself was tempted in that which He has suffered, He is able to come to the aid of those who are tempted."[3] He too was ready to get off the tracks. He too was ready to except God's deliverance. He too asked the Father one last time if there was a plan B. He knows the agony more than you or I ever will.

And because he is so familiar with the pain, he is so present to comfort. And because cross-bearing powerfully magnifies my experiential need for his presence, I search for it and cling to it like never before.

Do you want to really know Jesus? Take up your cross and you will meet him in a way you could not have anticipated. Walk in his footsteps and you will discover a sweetness of his abiding presence that is unique, surprising and sufficient.

Or you could settle for pity.

But the absence of pity for cross-bearers is not correlated to the absence of pain. A cross-bearer does not require pity because a cross-bearer has discovered that the quality of fellowship found

1. Phil 3:10.
2. 2 Cor 1:5.
3. Heb 2:18.

with Jesus far outweighs whatever pain was endured to find it. To discover Jesus in my darkest hour has become a gift that I would not forgo.

Do not weep for me, I go to meet with him. He is the joy set before me.

"For to you it has been granted for Christ's sake, not only to believe in Him, but also to suffer for His sake."[4] You have been handed a divinely ordained opportunity, a VIP all-access pass. Jesus is there, in the midst of human suffering, beckoning you to join him.

Few learned this like Peter. Read his first letter to the believers. The message is there throughout.

> For this finds favor, if for the sake of conscience toward God a person bears up under sorrows when suffering unjustly. . . . For you have been called for this purpose, since Christ also suffered for you, leaving you an example for you to follow in His steps, who committed no sin, nor was any deceit found in His mouth; and while being reviled, He did not revile in return; while suffering, He uttered no threats, but kept entrusting Himself to Him who judges righteously. (1 Pet 2:19, 21–23)

> But even if you should suffer for the sake of righteousness, you are blessed. and do not fear their intimidation, and do not be troubled, . . . For it is better, if God should will it so, that you suffer for doing what is right rather than for doing what is wrong. (1 Pet 3:14, 17)

> Therefore, those also who suffer according to the will of God shall entrust their souls to a faithful Creator in doing what is right. (1 Pet 4:19)

The man who couldn't deal, the friend who couldn't come to terms, finally came to terms with the role of suffering in the ministry of Jesus and his followers. "They went on their way from the presence of the Council, rejoicing that they had been considered worthy to suffer shame for His name" (Acts 5:41).

4. Phil 1:29.

Peter had discovered a fellowship with his friend and Savior through suffering that was of a different quality than the fellowship he had previously experienced. Not meaningless suffering, but redemptive suffering. He not only valued that fellowship, he felt compelled to point others to it. This truth produced a joy in his heart that could not be contained.

Through his writings, Peter is the friend to us that he failed to be with Jesus. Peter is now the friend who encourages us to stay the course when we suffer. He does not offer the strong protection he once offered Jesus. He does not suggest we are too important for this. He offers no pity.

Peter challenges us to embrace suffering as the inevitable outcome of saying yes to Jesus. In doing so, Peter redefines what it means to be a friend within the context of cross-bearing. The guy who unwittingly sided with Satan now sides with Jesus and together they invite you to take up your cross.

There will come a time, maybe many, when you will want to fight back, or get away, and Jesus calls you to go along. But you will never be alone. Jesus will always and forever meet you there with his power and peace. So look for him. Seek him out. His fellowship will be sweetest when most necessary.

Meeting him is but a foretaste of the joy set before.

This was always plan A.

PRACTICUM
The People

Chapter 6

ADVISING

A TEMPLATE FOR PASTORAL COUNSEL

I realize many things have changed over 2,000 years, but I still wonder how Jesus did ministry without coffee shops. Surely the synagogues of the day served a hot beverage to their visitors. I have had so many profound moments at coffee shops, it just seems there must have been an ancient equivalent.

One summer morning found me sitting across a small, three-legged table from a young man not long married. As we each sipped on our cup of joe, he told the story of his wife's infidelity. He was heartbroken as he spoke and I was heartbroken as I listened. Beyond the pain of it was the deep sense of uncertainty. This man did not know if his wife wanted to stay married or leave. He was in search of clarity.

After sharing his sad tale, he had only one question for me, "Should I stay married or should I leave?" Yikes. That is a high-stakes question. The options of leaving or staying are both laden with heartache and challenges. Given his situation, those will both be painful options. What to do?

Well, like a good pastor, I start with the Bible. God's word has some things to say about divorce. In this man's case, his wife has breached the covenant of marriage and divorce would be both permissible and understandable.[1] But God also hates divorce[2] and this could be an opportunity to incarnate God's heart for redemption. Should he get away or go along?

There will be many similar conversations over the course of your tenure in pastoral ministry. A hurting soul is at the crossroads of two painful options and can't decide what to do. For the inexperienced shepherd, this feels like a minefield. I certainly don't want to be the responsible party when things inevitably become even more difficult and I certainly don't have any magical powers by which I could fix the heartache. In my younger years I would freeze at this point, unable to move in any direction with confidence.

But Jesus already gave a way forward. It is the same path that he took and the one that you are currently on. It is the summary cost analysis for anyone wishing to be a disciple of Jesus, deny yourself, take up your cross and follow Me. Three simple directives that provide a way forward for any person standing at the crossroads.

First, deny yourself. To deny myself is to decide that regardless of the hardship, I am not now going to make decisions out of self-interest. Self-denial in this case is not self-deprecation. It is the Gethsemane prayer of not my will but yours. I will not place my own considerations at the forefront and explain that decision with my pain. I will acknowledge the pain and submit my will to God's. "God, in my own will I want this cup taken from me. But I want Your will even more."

A man betrayed feels very justified in making it about himself and his pain. That seems reasonable. But self-preservation is not the pathway to the greatest joy. As he stands at the crossroads of painful divorce and painful reconciliation, he must be able to say "Not my will, but yours be done." God's will must take precedence.

Then, take up your cross. The cup that Jesus asked to be removed from him was the cup of the cross. It was the cup of carrying

---

1. Matt 19:9: "And I say to you, whoever divorces his wife, except for sexual immorality, and marries another woman commits adultery."

2. Mal 2:16a: "'For I hate divorce,' says the LORD, the God of Israel."

the sin and suffering of the world on his own shoulders. It wasn't his cross to bear, it was ours. And when the Father reminded the Son of his will, he went along and carried the burden that we could not carry on our own.

To take up a cross is to make myself available to bear up under suffering that is not my own. "But why do I have to repay what I did not steal?"[3] Why do I have to repair what I did not destroy? Because it is the way of Jesus. It is the way of love.

Once this young man has agreed to place the will of God at the center of his decision-making, there is another difficult step. He must now decide if he is willing to suffer for the sake of his wife's redemption. He must now decide if he is willing to drink the painful cup. To take up your cross is to pursue a benefit for another person at great cost to yourself.

But not all opportunities to take up your cross for another should be accepted. Remember, there were plenty of times when Jesus got away. It wasn't time. Is it time for this young man to get away or go along? That is exactly the question he is asking me. And that is exactly the question I cannot emphatically answer.

But God can. The third piece of the template is the invitation "follow me." Only the Spirit of God knows what the outcome of staying or leaving will be. Only he knows the trajectory of this relationship. Only he can speak to this young man and lead him. And only a person ready to deny self and carry a cross can hear him.

Inviting another person onto the pathway of Jesus is one of the most difficult and important conversations a shepherd will ever have. "For all that is in the world—the lust of the flesh, lust of the eyes, and the boastful pride of life—comes not from the Father but from the world."[4] It is all a lie. The one who wishes to save his life must lose it.[5]

In one of the final conversations Jesus had with his good friend, he expressed confidence that Peter would follow this

---

3. Ps 69:4.

4. John 2:16.

5. Matt 16:25: "For whoever wants to save his life will lose it; but whoever loses his life for My sake will find it."

path. Jesus knew Peter the cross-denier would become Peter the cross-bearer.

> "Truly, truly I tell you, when you were younger, you used to put on your belt and walk wherever you wanted; but when you grow old, you will stretch out your hands and someone else will put your belt on you and bring you where you do not want to go." Now He said this, indicating by what kind of death he would glorify God. And when He had said this, He said to him, "Follow Me!"[6]

And so, to the man with a cup of coffee getting cold for lack of attention, I extend this invitation. First, as tempting as it may be right now, do not make this about you. Seek God's will. Second, accept that God has called you to suffer for his redemptive purposes. And lastly, follow him. No matter what, follow Jesus. He will show you what to do.

As I leave the café and head for my pickup, I am deeply aware of the difficulty of my words. He cannot do it alone. He may decide not to do it at all. But if only he could catch a glimpse of the joy set before him, he would scorn the shame of it all. And that is my prayer for him.

6. John 21:18–19.

Chapter 7

TERMINATION AND ALIENATION

HOSTILE MINISTRY RELATIONSHIPS

As a child of overseas missionaries, I remember hearing rumors of another missionary family that had left the field. The rumor was that the husband had suffered a nervous breakdown and would return to the US to get well. For the missionary community that meant one thing; we would never see that family again.

Shepherding ministry in a local community is a different arrangement. There will be those who don't make it in vocational ministry for any number of reasons. Eventually you will have to let someone go. But they do not return to their homeland to get well. You get to bump into that person at the local grocery every week for the next twenty years. He or she may even decide to continue attending your church for fellowship or for lack of a better option.

The mechanics of ministry terminations require a long view of relationships and cross-bearing as a centralizing principle.

Jesus offered two options in the face of persecution or hostility, get away or go along. Remember, there was no fight-back option. But this simply cannot mean that a shepherd must agree to go along with or runaway from every problematic person in ministry. There would be no long-game pastors if this were the case. So how do we understand cross-bearing in this context?

The first challenge most shepherds face is in relationship to a superior. The general track of vocational ministry has young talent filling subordinate roles as they gather experience and skill in leadership. If relational challenges surface early on, it is usually in relationship to a person with oversight, not a subordinate.

Young pastors may find themselves at odds with a senior pastor, an elder, or a board of some kind. This narrative is all too common. As a subordinate, you have certain duties and boundaries placed upon your authority. There may be things that you want to change about your church, and they may be things that should change. But as a subordinate, you do not possess explicit authority to bring about those changes. So, what do you do? Maybe you test the waters of willingness with the leader you trust the most. You offer the insight you have in order to discover if there is an open door to usher in the change you desire.

And for many, this is where things first take a sour turn. Early in ministry, these conversations were probably marked more by youthful enthusiasm than by tactful wisdom. But regardless of the rationale, the door is closed. And because you are now on record with your viewpoint, you can't walk it back. You have outed yourself.

The unfortunate reality is that some church superiors do not know how to encourage and guide healthy dialogue with true diversity of thought. Once you have spoken your mind, you may become suspect. But remember, this is not about them, this is about you. What are your two options? You can get away or go along. And there are a few ways to discern God's will in this decision.

The first is an employment agreement. If you agreed to stay for a certain time period, I would suggest, barring gross immorality and even to your own detriment, you stick it out and meet Christ in that difficult place.[1] Let him teach you how to be reviled without reviling. Practice going two miles when you shouldn't have to go one. Your fleshly nature will hate it. But the dying will produce wonderful fruit in your life if you let it.

---

1. Ps 15:4b: "But he honors those who fear the LORD; He takes an oath to his own detriment, and does not change."

Another indicator that will help you make your decision is when your superior makes it known that he or she wants you gone. If your superior is throwing spears, it may be time to get away.[2] Even if you want to stay. And it doesn't really matter if most people in your church would side with you against your superior. You want the ministry the Father grants you, not the ministry you grasped for yourself.[3] Accept that you are under authority and decide to honor the guidance of that authority with grace and humility. Get away. And throw no spears on your way out.

The deeply personal challenge in these types of situations begins with the realization that I only really have control over my own heart. I want desperately to control other factors even if I don't consciously acknowledge that desire. I want the best for this ministry and I want to be a part of a ministry that doesn't embarrass me. But I have not been given that decision-making power. The authority to do so is not invested in my position. So I am left with the much more difficult and humble task of dealing with my own heart before God.[4]

For this reason, these situations are ripe with opportunity for fruit bearing. Take up your cross.

Probably the more complicated situation is cross-bearing in the context of hostile subordinates. As a superior, you do have power that must be appropriately wielded. To refuse to use that power is an abdication of your responsibilities as one in authority. Furthermore, unaddressed toxicity in any ministry environment will have multiplied long-term effects. A loving shepherd always protects the sheep.[5]

Remember, the first step toward cross-bearing is self-denial.[6] Would-be shepherds get tripped up by hostile subordinates when

2. 1 Sam 18:11.

3. 1 Sam 24:6.

4. Ps 139:23–24: "Search me, God, and know my heart; Put me to the test and know my anxious thoughts; And see if there is any hurtful way in me, And lead me in the everlasting way."

5. John 10:11–15.

6. Matt 16:24: "Then Jesus said to His disciples, 'If anyone wants to come after Me, he must deny himself, take up his cross, and follow Me.'"

they take their attacks personally. Self-defense mechanisms can kick in before you are even aware of them. But if your cross-bearing is not about them, then it is also true that their cross-bearing is not ultimately about you. Subordinates become hostile for many reasons. When they handle their hostilities poorly it may be because they do not understand cross-bearing. They do not yet grasp that a person can be technically correct and morally wrong.

Hostile subordinates can be addressed in one of two ways, get away or go along. To go along with a hostile subordinate is to decide, with God's input, that working with this person's immaturities is part of God's plan for me. So I commit to stay involved in his or her maturation process. To be effective in this role, I must refuse to make the immaturities about me. I must maintain a constant eye toward the subordinate's growth by offering equal doses of grace and truth. My prayer through this is "Father, forgive them, they know not what they do."

To shepherd hostile subordinates is to accept that some of their arrows are going to sting. But I also believe that because of God's work in my life, I am uniquely qualified to absorb those painful barbs in pursuit of true deliverance. I want to see this person free. Despite the pain they cause, I decide, at least for now, to go along rather than get away. I do not agree with the bad behavior, but I am going to show patience toward the process of growth and ask for God's intervening work. I choose not to start a fight. And if this person rejects my input, I am not alone in that experience.[7]

But sometimes the fallout is too great. Sometimes a shepherd must respond to a subordinate's hostility by getting away. The subtle nuance between getting away and fighting back is critical. To get away by dismissing an employee is a severe mercy. Firing a toxic team member in the context of cross-bearing requires a couple of firm convictions.

---

7. Isa 6:9: "And He said, 'Go, and tell this people: "Keep on listening, but do not understand; And keep on looking, but do not gain knowledge."'"

Matt 13:13: "Therefore I speak to them in parables; because while seeing they do not see, and while hearing they do not hear, nor do they understand."

First, the dismissal is not about my own self-preservation. My motivation is equally the health of my organization and the health of my hostile subordinate. The two concerns operate in tandem. According to the prophet Samuel, insubordination is akin to devil worship[8] and the devil never has good intentions for those who unwittingly follow his commands.[9] Throughout the process of necessary warning steps along with remediation opportunities, I must never lose my desire to see this person mature. Even in the final moment, when all options have been exhausted, I remain sincerely hopeful[10] that through dismissal, this person I love will be confronted with the need to change.

Second, I must always act and speak toward this hostile subordinate in a way that opens the door for future reconciliation. I will not be the one to slam it shut. Jesus calls me to act toward this person with the same self-sacrificing love that he showed me. So I will be gentle, and humble in heart. The next time I see this former subordinate at the local grocer, I will not be ashamed to offer a greeting because I have consistently acted toward him or her as Jesus would.

Lastly, termination is a role change, not necessarily a family change. The factors that disqualify a person from a position of authority may not exclude that same person from fellowship within the family of God. Alienating a subordinate from the fellowship of his or her church family may cut them off from the resources necessary for continued growth. But when I act with grace and truth, I ensure that I do not make myself the reason for my subordinate's alienation. I will not make it weird. This is especially critical in the context of small community where other fellowship options are limited.

No matter the challenge, I refuse to fight back. I refuse to act punitively. I refuse to take it personally and cast myself as a victim.

---

8. 1 Sam 15:23a: "For rebellion is as reprehensible as the sin of divination, and insubordination is as reprehensible as false religion and idolatry. "

9. John 10:10a: "The thief comes only to steal and kill and destroy."

10. 1 Cor 13:7: "[Love] keeps every confidence, it believes all things, hopes all things, endures all things."

I refuse to allow another person's bad behavior to take my eye off the redemptive ministry of cross-bearing. In fact, my commitment to the crucified life is only further awakened and strengthened in the face of this adversity.

As far as I am concerned, the opportunity for forgiveness-based fellowship has not in any way been diminished. I do not demand it, but I offer it. I simply cannot stand before the crucified Savior and explain my own unwillingness to extend my arms of forgiveness and love.[11] My desire for forgiveness is no less for those who would pound the nails, than for those who watch in helpless agony.

And in this moment, you become the shepherd. Through cross-bearing you show the only pathway to true community and invite the flock to join you. All for the joy set before us.

The decision to get away or go along is a tricky one. It requires you to deny yourself and take up your cross. Only then can you fully follow him. He must lead you moment by moment.

Now let's address those who's hostility was on record even before they walked in your doors.

11. Matt 18:21–35.

Chapter 8

CENTURIONS
WELCOMING REPENTANT HOSTILES

A number of events surrounding the death of Jesus on the cross are described in far too little detail in the Gospels. Darkness in the afternoon, earthquakes, dead saints walking out of their graves; it is all very strange. But there is one detail in the narrative of Matt 27 that presents a particularly complex riddle for the early church.

As the supernatural events unfolded, a particular centurion of the Roman army had been tasked, along with a small cohort, with standing guard at the crucifixion grounds. Their senses told them this was no ordinary criminal hanging from the pole. So disturbing and terrifying was the scene, the Roman soldiers made a confession of belief: "Truly this was the Son of God!"[1]

The same narrative tells us there were other groups present as well. Some of the disciples, Jesus's dearest and closest friends, were there. Mary Magdalene was there along with the mother of James and John, and Mary the mother of Jesus. Many others who were involved and engaged in the ministry of Jesus were there. And the Roman soldiers.

Imagine for a moment this scene unfolding several months later: the followers of Jesus all gathered for fellowship in celebration

---

1. Mark 15:39.

of the gift of righteousness and God's Spirit, joy and love abounding by the fruit of his Spirit. And in walks the centurion. "Wait, why do I recognize him? Where have I seen him before?" And just as their minds place him at the scene of Jesus' brutal death, he utters these words: "I believe."

On the one hand the body of Christ, the kingdom of heaven, is large enough to include all those who trust Jesus and are made alive through his Spirit.[2] On the other hand, this guy is a Roman. And not just any Roman, he is a Roman soldier. And not just any soldier, but a centurion in the Roman army, a man in charge. And not just any Roman centurion, but the Roman centurion who oversaw the murder of our innocent leader!

On the one hand he was just doing his job. How could he know any better? He was raised a Roman and was acting consistently with his training, his status, his culture, and his upbringing. On the other hand, he is a willing contributor to the brutal rule of the oppressor class. And did we mention, he lent his hand to crucify the only begotten Son of God?!

Pastoral ministry in community life will lead you into a similar predicament. At some point, the preacher of the gospel will stand face to face with a centurion looking for fellowship. The centurion will take one of any number of different forms, but the basic profile is a person who previously caused harm to you or your church and now wants to be embraced as part of the flock.

The first part of this question is fairly straight forward. Both Jesus and Paul led by example and welcomed oppressors into fellowship without hesitation. Paul joyfully baptized his jailer's entire family[3] and Jesus commended a centurion's great faith.[4] They both gave flesh to the prayer of Jesus: "Father, forgive them for they know not what they do."

---

2. Gal 3:28: "There is neither Jew nor Greek, there is neither slave nor free, there is neither male nor female; for you are all one in Christ Jesus."

3. Acts 16:25–30.

4. Matt 8:10: "Now when Jesus heard this, He was amazed and said to those who were following, 'Truly I say to you, I have not found such great faith with anyone in Israel.'"

But the more complicated issue has to do with involvement in church ministry. Should a person who previously caused harm be permitted into ministry leadership? The answer to this question is often related to the severity of the pain the perpetrator caused the pastor. Pastors without a proper understanding of cross-bearing may be tempted to behave punitively, wanting the perpetrator to get a dose of the pain that he or she caused. This attitude is rooted in resentment. Deny yourself.

Over years of pastoral ministry, I have known harmful people who eventually returned and sought fellowship, even leadership. To be more precise, these were people who were harmful to me, who now want to be embraced into the fellowship I lead. Often the bad behaviors were behaviors the person learned in a different environment where dysfunction and self-preservation were the norm. The longer they lived or worked in an anti-gospel context, the more deeply rooted the bad behaviors.

Sometimes the harm they caused was through malice and gossip. They might not even know that I am aware of their words. But I am. And in that moment, I am deeply tempted to want to make it briefly about me. I want them to know the hurt they caused for my own satisfaction.

Can you imagine meeting the resurrected Savior face-to-face for the first time and discovering that he wants first to focus on the pain that you caused? "Do you know what a lousy follower you were?" What an awkward greeting.

Once committed to absorbing painful barbs through redemptive cross-bearing, my response to formerly harmful people is still a bit tricky. I should deeply desire for this harmful person to know God's forgiveness. But I have a responsibility to the flock, to ensure that immature, harmful, or even toxic people are not given opportunities for influence. Here are a few guiding principles:

Proceed with caution. I appreciate the response of the disciples to the newly converted Saul. Can you imagine someone showing up at your church who was previously arresting and murdering your members?! This is the guy who was "breathing threats and murder."[5] It was his oxygen. Hesitancy to embrace him seems warranted. "When he came to Jerusalem, he was trying to associate with the disciples; but they were all afraid of him, not believing that he was a disciple."[6]

Talk it out. After some initial hesitancy, Saul and the church leaders were able to sit down and have a meaningful conversation about Saul's past and Saul's conversion. A mutual friend facilitated the sit-down. "But Barnabas took hold of him and brought him to the apostles and described to them how he had seen the Lord on the road, and that He had talked to him."[7] When the time is right, it's good to talk it out: "Let's address your history and hear your testimony of how God has changed you." If forgiveness needs to be extended, now is the time.

Look for fruit. Barnabas went on to tell the disciples "how at Damascus he had spoken out boldly in the name of Jesus."[8] True repentance is always followed by fruit in that person's life.[9] To look for fruit is not to put this person on public trial. It is not the ministry of skepticism and nursing old wounds. It is the honoring and gracious work of confirming the outward evidences of the Spirit's internal work, the same Spirit that works in me.

If love hopes in all things, it hopes that your former persecutors can be restored. It's not complicated. It's just very difficult to love the crucifier in a hopeful manner.

If a former murderer can become an apostle, it is likely that the former jerk who acted contemptuously toward you can become a small group leader.

Wisdom and discernment suggest that allowing sufficient time for observation is critical before making decisions about how a formerly hostile person will be integrated into your church body. It is okay to wonder if the conversion is real, if the transformation

---

5. Acts 9:1.

6. Acts 9:26.

7. Acts 9:27a.

8. Acts 9:27b.

9. Matt 3:8: "Therefore produce fruit consistent with repentance."

is permanent. It is okay to be cautious. Just so long as your caution is not rooted in the self-serving desire to prove a point.

Saul turned out to be quite an asset to the church and to us. I'm thankful the disciples eventually embraced him into their fellowship. I'm thankful they gave Saul the opportunity to address and repent of his prior training.

Religiosity destroyed him. The gospel set him free. The church took him in. And he went on to write a portion of the Bible.

Now imagine Saul accepting salvation and stalling out in his sanctification.

Chapter 9

POWER PLAYERS
REFUSING UNREPENTANT CROSS-DENIERS

It requires a tremendous amount of inner strength to offer a formerly harmful person a seat at the table. Only truly transformed leaders will have sufficient humility and grace. But there are some who should not be given a seat under any circumstances.

In chapter 7 I addressed how a pastor should respond when getting away is the only option. To get away from a hostile superior or subordinate requires wisdom and discernment from God. But there are issues other than hostility. Certain potential leaders should never be put in charge.

I'll assume that my experience is common and suggest that every pastor is going to have to resist the efforts of harmful and unrepentant would-be leaders. These are people who would like to be invited into leadership but lack the key ingredients necessary for shepherding ministry. They may express their interest to you in explicit terms or they might tell everyone but you that they deserve to be in leadership. You should get away.

Jesus was approached by unqualified men who wanted to be part of his inner circle. But he wasn't having it. Rather than getting in deep with these guys, he called it from the get-go: "Nope, you are not qualified. You do not have what it takes to take on a role of shepherding influence."[1]

This is an interesting judgment call for Jesus to make. After all, the men he invited into his inner circle had sufficient problems of their own. They got it wrong a lot. But there were some problems Jesus was willing to work with, and others he was not.

Using "Deny yourself, take up your cross, and follow me" as a guide, I'd like to offer a few trademarks of would-be leaders that you should avoid allowing into positions of influence.

I'll rise to the occasion. These are leaders who do not show fruit in their own lives consistent with the shepherding ministry. They are not cross-bearers. They are not disciple makers. They seem lukewarm. But, if you gave them a position, of course they would plan to develop those traits and behaviors. In fact, a few people who know them are very confident that if you offered them a position of influence, that would be the secret ingredient to unlocking their potential. But Jesus' invitation was to forfeit everything as a precondition of following.[2] Granting authority as a means of prompting someone's motivation seems risky to me. My experience has been that this promotes an environment where position is more important that transformation.

I can fix every problem. This is the leader who knows exactly what the problems are with your church, knows exactly what needs to be done to fix those problems, and has no need for your input on the matter. Opinions are expressed as certainties, contrary evidence is ignored, and questions are never asked. They often demonstrate a profound lack of curiosity. It's all so obvious, only an idiot would disagree. When you finally get a clue, you will put this genius in charge. The lack of intellectual humility will become toxic, and a wildly successful track record of for-profit business acumen is irrelevant. This leader does not deny self or follow but insists, "Deny *yourself*, and follow Me!" Get away.

Why are you attacking me? This leader does not dominate others with a sharp intellect but instead wields the power of their

1. Luke 9:57–62.
2. Matt 4:18–22.

49

own internal victimization narrative. If he or she is called out in any substantial way, it is immediately personal because you are contributing to this narrative. You will hear this kind of leader say things like "Why are you upset with me?" or "Why are you doing this to me?" A lack of validation is interpreted as a personal beef. You are not allowed to simply disagree over facts. And if you insist in your disagreement, this leader will respond with something like "I am sorry I offended you." The apology is insincere, intended to evoke your pity. This leader does not obey the command to "deny yourself." This leader constantly places self at the center of everything. Get away.

There are two criteria that I instinctively invoke when selecting leaders. First, can this person materially benefit my ministry in some way? Second, will this person embarrass me in some way? I can easily take a utilitarian approach. Jesus took on young men who had little to offer other than enthusiasm, and because of their enthusiasm, constantly acted in embarrassing ways consistent with their immaturity. "Lord, do you want us to call down fire?!"[3] Um, no. But he saw potential and committed to form them into cross-bearing shepherds.

As an aside, a pious aversion to formal leadership roles is not a qualification for leadership and a desire for leadership is not a disqualifier.[4] "Well, he doesn't want the job so he really has the right heart." This feels like contradictory nonsense. The person who loves giving and serving would not be barred from giving and serving. Why bar leaders who love leading? Gifted leaders *should* be motivated by desire, not compulsion.[5]

If I am to fulfill my calling as a cross-bearing shepherd, I must make disciples, showing others how to take up a cross and follow

---

3. Luke 9:54: "When His disciples James and John saw this, they said, 'Lord, do You want us to command fire to come down from heaven and consume them?'"

4. 1 Tim 3:1: "This saying is trustworthy: 'If anyone aspires to be an overseer, he desires a noble work.'"

5. 1 Pet 5:2: "Shepherd the flock of God among you, exercising oversight, not under compulsion but voluntarily, according to the will of God; and not with greed but with eagerness."

Jesus. What I am really looking for, if I want a ministry characterized by resurrection life, is men and women who are drawn to cross-bearing. "Do not come unless you can say to your Lord and to us, *The Cross is the attraction.*"[6]

Peter resisted cross-bearing and yet placed himself firmly under the leadership of Jesus. Jesus knew it would be a hard-learned lesson but he was confident that Peter would figure it out. He knew Peter would learn to bear a cross.

Other potential leaders Jesus quickly identified as persistent cross-deniers. And there was no future in ministry with Jesus for cross-deniers. He quickly got away from these types. And you should too. For now. If they change their ways and accept the ministry of cross-bearing, refer to chapter 8.

6. Amy Carmichael, as quoted in Elisabeth Elliot, *A Chance to Die: The Life and Legacy of Amy Carmichael* (Grand Rapids, MI: Revell, 2005), 265.

Chapter 10

NOBODY CALLED

THE SUBTLE MANIPULATION OF EXPERIMENTAL ABANDONMENT

If I told you that one of my young children, fed up with my flawed authority, hit the road in search of greener pasture, you would understand. You might even find it humorous and endearing. Plenty of kids have stated their intent to find a more agreeable family situation, packed their bags and marched down the driveway.

But, if I told you that I, fed up with my flawed children, had hit the road in search of greener pasture, you would be rightfully concerned. Not because this doesn't happen. But when you are an adult, it is no longer cute, it is very consequential.

I have heard a line, said by people who have left the church, many times over many years. My church leaders have heard the same line many times over many years. It feels like a gut punch every time. And yet my emotional reaction is a very confused mix of sad, angry, and what I can only describe as some version of "yuck."

The line goes like this: "Yeah, I haven't been to church in like five weeks and nobody even bothered to call me."

First, I feel sad. Feeling alone is the first and worst kind of human experience. God looked down at his perfect creation and said, "It is not good for man to be alone."[1] We need friends. We need

1. Gen 2:18.

connection. We need to care and be cared for. Anytime someone describes being lonely it hurts my heart. I know the feeling and it is a deeply painful one.

But I am not just sad because this person doesn't have good connections at church. I am sad because this person hasn't *made* good connections at church which leads me to believe they do not know *how* to make those connections at church. I understand relationships are a two-way street and this person is parked in a cul-de-sac.

And this is the part that makes me a little angry. I feel defensive in response to what is usually an underhanded slight against the people of my church, particularly my leaders. The implication is that it was our job to provide a sense of meaningful connection and we failed at our job. On the one hand, I truly feel bad that it happened this way. On the other hand, I feel as though an apology would lend credence to the underlying lie—"My relational needs are your responsibility."

What to do?

Well, first I need to deal with the yuck. The yuck I feel is in response to self-serving self-righteousness disguised as victimization. Is there any other context where it would be relationally acceptable for me to abandon a person and then blame that person for not doing enough to reconcile my abandonment? "Yes, I left. But you should have called!" It feels very juvenile. How does anyone defend such a manipulative mindset?

As it turns out, they use Scripture.

> And so He told them this parable, saying, "What man among you, if he has a hundred sheep and has lost one of them, does not leave the other ninety-nine in the open pasture and go after the one that is lost, until he finds it? And when he has found it, he puts it on his shoulders, rejoicing.
> And when he comes home, he calls together his friends and his neighbors, saying to them, "Rejoice with me, because I have found my sheep that was lost!" (Luke 15:3–6)

You see, a pastor who is like Jesus would leave the flock and go searching for the one that had wandered away. A pastor who is like Jesus cares more about the one, than the many. And for a period of time, I bought this fallacy and the guilt it induced.

But there is more to the story. Jesus told this story to the Pharisees, to the self-righteous, self-serving Pharisees. This story is meant to reveal the broken motives of the listener. Hear how the story ends:

> I tell you that in the same way, there will be more joy in heaven over one sinner who repents than over ninety-nine righteous people who have no need of repentance. (Luke 15:7)

The one Jesus went after was the sinner aware of the need for repentance. The ninety-nine that he left behind were the self-righteous, self-serving Pharisees who did not see in themselves any sin or wrong sufficient to warrant repentance. He rejoiced not because he located a wandering sheep. He rejoiced because a sheep cried out in need of a savior. And heaven rejoiced in the same.

I do not lay out the meaning of this parable to condemn the person who says "Nobody called." I lay out the meaning of this parable to remove condemnation from the pastor who feels that cross-bearing involves chasing after people who take no responsibility for themselves. It is not your fault that the person who makes no effort to reach out to friends has friends that make no effort to reach out.

Just as you should never put the love of others to the test, they should not put your love to the test or that of your church. It is not just self-serving; it is always ultimately self-deceiving. You cannot experience love this way. It doesn't work. And as long as this mindset persists, they will not find the love they seek.

The challenge for me as a shepherd is to engage this person with truth and grace while keeping my own ego at bay. Nothing awakens my own self-righteousness like self-righteousness. Especially when served up with an underhanded and unfair accusation. What they want to make my fault, I want to make theirs.

The situation requires compassion but a compassion that does not agree with the lie this person believes. My compassion is *because* of the lie that he or she believes. It is not good to be alone, no matter the underlying cause.

"I'm really sorry to hear that. Feeling unseen or uncared for is always so painful. Is there some way that I could help you build stronger relationships at our church so that you feel more connected in the future? Have you considered joining a small group?" Compassion should take a constructive approach.

And to the pastors who have carried that false burden, it's not your fault. I know, it feels yuck to be blamed. If feels yuck to have someone imply that your church is an unfriendly place. But you do not have to take that on.

Love your flock. Pursue those that go astray. And when some fall through the cracks, graciously point them back and send them on their way.

Chapter 11

WISH YOU COULD STAY

RESPONDING TO DEPARTURES WITH APPROPRIATE GRACE AND GRIEF

Although cross-bearers are often called to endure hostility, there is always a sigh of relief when God either grants us permission to get away or sends the hostile person away. I am thankful for the lessons learned but rarely so thankful as to wish this difficult person would continue to cause me grief.

But there is another kind of ministry departure that will eventually become a source of grief for every shepherd. The disciples of Jesus knew this grief well. They had experienced the heartache of parting ways with not only a close friend and confidant, but a man who was the heartbeat of their ministry. None of them could envision a ministry going forward without Jesus.

There will come a day in shepherding ministry when a dear friend will announce his or her departure. Not just a dear friend, but a dear friend who has fundamentally shaped your ministry. This is not a finger or a toe member of the body. This is a backbone or maybe a heart kind of person. Just as this member profoundly influenced your ministry for good, their departure will be experienced as a tremendous loss. You cannot imagine your ministry without this individual present.

These announcements are never anything short of a gut punch. But shouldering the grief of these departures with grace is an essential skill for a cross-bearing shepherd. Getting it wrong in these vulnerable moments can cause long-lasting harm. So here are some tips:

Why are doing this to me? I know many stories of departures that became personal offenses, whether to a pastor or an employer from some other field. To the degree that the employee or leader is valuable, they are not permitted the option of leaving without first receiving an emotional bludgeoning. It isn't possible that God is simply leading in a new direction. "If you leave, you are deserting me and my ministry. You are wounding us by your decision. You should feel bad." If this message isn't made explicit, it is powerfully implied.

This sentiment is as appalling as it is common. And it reveals a pastor-centric shepherding framework. The ministry subordinates are valuable only insofar as they facilitate the pastor's vision and plans. This is not cross-bearing leadership. This is crown-wearing ministry. Your flock soon realizes their value is connected to their value to *your* ministry. Continue to serve the pastor and all is good. Decide to leave, and the king will be unhappy. And this unhappiness is often expressed with mountains of guilt.

As a cross-bearing shepherd, I must never attach my people's allegiance to me or my ministry. No one owes me anything. The purpose of my ministry is to attach them to God. He knows best how they are to be used for his purposes in the establishment of his kingdom. And when God moves the pieces on the board, sending a dear friend on to the next assignment, I trust his leading whatever the grief and I celebrate the time I was given with this valuable asset.

My people do not belong to me, they belong to God. My people do not serve my vision, they serve God's. My people are not accountable to me for understanding their life purpose, they are accountable to God. When he shares some of the best ones with me for a short while, I praise him for his kindness. When they leave, I endure the cross of grief with grace, for the joy set before me.

Hey, it's no big deal! Once you have committed to graciously releasing those that God is sending somewhere else, it is important not to overstate your permission-granting kindness. In your efforts to avoid making a departing team member feel guilty about their departure, some leaders go too far and inadvertently come across as indifferent or worse, happy about it.

The goal is to simultaneously hold and express joy for their future and grief for their departure. You want the exiting member to know you are sad because of their great value to the kingdom of God, and you are excited because of their great value to the kingdom of God. You can experience both. And to the degree you love the person, you will.

It was the cross that set us free. Cross-bearing shepherds are always setting others free to love and follow God. When people depart your ministry, they should leave free. Your best nursery worker is stepping out because her five children have all graduated the ministry. She should leave feeling valued, honored, and free. Your lead sound engineer is stepping down because he wants to focus on serving at the local food pantry. He should leave feeling valued, honored, and free. Your youth pastor has been offered a lead pastor position in a neighboring community. He should leave feeling valued, honored, and free. No debts, no guilt, no shame, no outstanding obligations or unspoken expectations. It is for freedom that Christ set them free.[1] So let them walk in it.

And when you hear of their remarkable success as part of another ministry, celebrate God's faithfulness with your flock and give testimony. When you celebrate those who have moved on to bigger and better things, you will set your members free from any defensiveness they may feel on your behalf. Just because you don't regard it as desertion, doesn't mean others won't. Show them a better way.

---

1. Gal 5:1.

When you make good investments in those who go on to serve in other places, your church becomes a blessing to the broader community and to the world.

Chapter 12

WHERE DID YOU GO?

THE VANISHING ACT OF POOR BOUNDARY SETTERS

There is another kind of painful departure that shepherds will navigate through the lifespan of ministry. This group of people is not leaving to take the next step in following God to the next thing. This group is not seeking your blessing as they open up a new chapter of pursuing God's calling. This group is mysterious and hard for shepherds to understand.

Your lead front-door greeter has been serving your church faithfully for seven years in that position. He is not needy, he is always willing to serve, and you have learned to rely on him to do the job well. You have only ever had very cordial conversations and you regard him as a model, selfless servant. And then, without warning, he disappears. A few weeks later you decide to check in with him and he seems as cordial as ever. When you mention his absence, he offers a vague apology but no context. Two months later, you bump into him again at the post office. He is warm, happy to see you as always, and enthusiastically explains that he has been invited to lead a men's small group at another church.

Your preschool Sunday school teacher is a twenty-three-year-old college graduate who moved back to town eighteen months ago. Her family has been a part of your church for years and from the time she was ten, she has been offering to help in the nursery. During her high school years, she was a star volunteer and the kids loved her contagious enthusiasm. Throughout her college years, she would return during the summers and jump right back into her role. Your children's ministry director mentions to you that this young woman declined her teaching role five weeks ago and hasn't responded to any of the volunteer invitations since. She has not been seen at church either. Two weeks later you bump into her mother and ask how her daughter is doing. She responds, "She's been pretty busy," but does not explain her absence. Nine months later, your star children's ministry volunteer shows back up to church and never mentions children's ministry again.

Part of the pain of these separations is rooted in your confusion about them. But a cross-bearing shepherd also recognizes that to sever relationship without explanation is dishonoring. It hurts because it isn't handled properly. So, what happened?

There will always be people in your ministry who are incompetent boundary setters. Joe is a very poor boundary setter. As Joe develops a growing distaste for his ministry role, he does not know how to express it. When asked how things are going, he only and always asserts that everything is fine. He does not want to disappoint anyone and he cannot bring himself to say "No." The reason he is such a valuable volunteer is because he is a poor boundary setter who agrees to whatever he is asked, not wanting to rock the boat.

At some point, Joe will reach his breaking point. His inner drive to keep the peace will eventually be overpowered by his desire to end his current assignment. This may take years, but it is inevitable. To avoid what he perceives will be a very awkward and guilt-inducing encounter, Joe will not tell you of his intended resignation. He will just disappear. If you call Joe to check in, he will engage as if everything is fine and normal. He doesn't want to talk about his disappearance. It is too difficult for him.

When this happens, it is natural to review your previous interactions with Joe and try to dissect what went wrong. Did I put too much pressure on him? Did I fail to express gratitude for his service? Did no one check in to see how he was feeling about his role? Was he given the freedom to change his role? The dilemma of this analysis is that you can always find fault in how Joe was handled and yet your mistakes do not explain his abrupt vanishment.

Joe disappeared because he cannot tell the truth when he fears it may disappoint someone. You can ask again and again and he will assure you that everything is fine. Then one day Joe is gone.

Your star children's ministry volunteer stopped enjoying children's ministry a long time ago. But she did not have the capacity to tell anyone. She would not limit her involvement by requesting a reduction in responsibilities. Instead, when she reached her breaking point, she vanished. She fled from the feeling of being a disappointment.

There are many ways you could unpack the subtle ironies of this dynamic. But your explanations and insight don't solve anything. The person who flees instead of implementing boundaries usually isn't looking to be lectured on the subject of internal inconsistencies. To raise this issue is to force the person into the very situation they will do almost anything to avoid, conflict.

Once you've opened the door and invited them to say what they want to say, let it go. Yes, it hurts. But take up your cross and scorn its shame. For the joy set before you.

Chapter 13

APPOINTMENTS

OFFENDED BY YOUR DIMINISHING AVAILABILITY

I remember sitting in my office one fall day many years ago when a critical observation first dawned upon the horizon of my mind. It was mid-afternoon and I was chatting with a young guy I had known for several years who had dropped in unannounced. Thirty minutes into our visit, it hit me; this guy is here in my office for only one reason, he is bored.

As a pastor, I regularly meet with people for all sorts of reasons. Some people are hurting and need encouragement. Some people are in trouble and need help. Some people are facing decisions and want guidance. And some people just want to hang out. When you shepherd in the context of a small community, hanging out is an important part of community life.

Around that same time, I heard an equipping session given by a megachurch pastor who talked about the importance of setting up boundaries around scheduling and limiting your members' unplanned direct access. From his vantage point, it made perfect sense. But I had already watched leaders implement similar measures in a way that seemed unnecessarily impersonal and alienating. When a pastor of a church of 100 handles appointments like the pastor of a church of 10,000, it feels off-putting.

I do not intend here to address the need for increasing levels of structured appointment making as your church grows. Many talks have been given on this. But shepherding leaders must learn to navigate the relational fallout that happens automatically as they become more intentional with their meetings schedule. As your church grows, you will naturally reach a point where you simply cannot meet all the demands. Not because you are unwilling, but because it is not mathematically possible.

When a new guest walks into your church and asks to meet with the pastor, the boundaries currently in place are generally accepted. New people rarely know what to expect when requesting a meeting with a pastor and are generally amicable to whatever schedule works for the pastor.

But not everyone is new to your church. Some have been there since the beginning. Some were there when the church was much smaller and felt more like a family effort. In the early stages, you did dinners together and coffee together and planning meetings together and Sundays together. But as the church grew, your inner circle also grew. And as your inner circle grew, it became increasingly cumbersome to have everyone present for every meeting and get together. So you acted accordingly.

As these early organically fluid experiences give way to more rigid structures, some people won't like it. Plenty of others get it, but some will not like it only because these changes have made you less available. Those who don't like your changing availability will fall into three categories. Some will leave your church because it has become "impersonal," some will tell others that they feel you have personally deserted them, and a very small number will address you directly with their concerns.

Regardless of how this discontentment is handled, shepherding leaders do not balk at this part of cross-bearing. Jesus too got in trouble for being unavailable.[1] The mature leader understands that what people are experiencing is a form of grief over loss—a loss that is beyond their control. Because they enjoy your company

---

1. John 11:21: "Martha then said to Jesus, 'Lord, if You had been here, my brother would not have died.'"

and are now forced to go without, this makes them feel sad and possibly hurt.

It will not be productive for you to respond defensively or with patronizing lectures about how you simply don't have time any more. You do have time. You have just chosen to manage your time differently and that decision comes with consequences. Now you must accept those consequences with grace.

First, when you love people, the separation will be a loss to you as well. And you will provide some balm to the hurting heart when you express this sadness. "I know it has been disappointing for you to drop into my office and repeatedly be told I'm unavailable. It has been hard for me too." It is okay to stick to your guns while owning both the practical and emotional outcomes of your decisions.

Second, you can be intentional even while less available. I find it hard to reach out to someone who I know is carrying disappointment directed toward me. But God does it all the time. Even though it will not solve the underlying unhappiness or hurt, it is a way of letting your friend know that he or she still matters and that you still care. "Hey, I know you stopped by my office a couple of times when I was tied up with another commitment. But I would love to connect! Is there a time next week that you would be free? If so, I'll put it on my calendar right now."

A shepherd who cares for others will respond to these disappointments with a gentle but firm hand. Not because it will solve the issue, but because it is the loving way. And when that person bails on you and your church anyway, carry that cross of grief without bitterness or resentment, for the joy set before you.

Chapter 14

FOREIGN FLOCKS

CARING FOR THOSE FROM OTHER MINISTRIES

The man on the other end of the line spoke in a hushed tone as he shared the sordid tale of his recently revealed indiscretions. He was hurting and broken while dealing with the hurt he had caused. As he finished the brief retelling of the fallout of the past few days, I asked him what he wanted from me. I asked this question because although this man is an acquaintance of mine, he attends a different church in town.

"I don't really want to talk to my pastor about this, or anyone else at my church for that matter . . . so I thought I would ask if you would be willing to help me." I understand that his comments are not so much a reflection of his church family, but of his own shame. He does not want the people he fellowships with every week to know his most damning secrets.

Now I have a dilemma. I always want to be able to help others; it's what I do. But my meeting schedule is already tight, limiting my ability to say yes. And this guy isn't even from my church. He has pastors and elders of his own that he does not want to turn to because of the sensitivity of his situation. This is one of those situations where the commonsense response seems straightforward: just say "no."

But I have another dilemma. As a cross-bearing shepherd, I have a duty to watch over my heart with all diligence. I have learned over time that it is not difficult for me to disguise self-serving tendencies as righteously motivated actions. And sometimes I disguise so well I fool myself. I make outwardly logical, good, smart decisions as a covert attempt to serve my own needs and build up my self-esteem.

If I'm being completely honest, I would admit that I am not motivated to make myself available to this man because there is no potential for his future involvement or contribution to my ministry. And I don't mean silly things like money or volunteer hours. I mean when this guy gets healed and whole in Jesus, he is going to be declaring his testimony of God's goodness . . . at some other church. If I dive in with him, the fruit of our hard-fought victories will ultimately belong to someone else's ministry.

If this explains my demotivation, the opposite supports my motivation. I am motivated to pursue ministry opportunities that will contribute to the overall forward movement of the ministry that I lead. I love to see a person transformed and I love for my church to receive all the benefits of that transformation. I am motivated to serve the success of my ministry. I am motivated by my success. I want to wear the crown, not bear the cross.

This phone call represents an opportunity to test my cross-bearing abilities. Cross-bearing is redemptive burden bearing. It is self-denial and self-sacrificing love. I could decline his request. I could get away. Or I could go along. I could say yes and invest some of my time and energy into a guy who has nothing to offer me or my ministry.

There will be many times when the answer to this phone call must be no. I must get away. But there will be times when the answer must be yes. Not because you have extra time. Because after denying yourself and taking up your cross, you committed to following Jesus. And in this case, Jesus led you to go along. You sought God in prayer and he said "Say yes" and so you said yes.

Once Jesus says yes, I engage this member of some other shepherd's flock. And right away I can tell if my joy over his growth is different than if he were one of my own. A lesser joy just means I still have work to do. God is still dealing with my heart, shaping it according to his priorities. I still have a ways to go.

As a cross-bearing shepherd, consider the benefit of spiritual foster care and seriously weigh each opportunity. Opportunities to grow in selflessness are a gift. So occasionally, say yes, and love them as your own.

Chapter 15

PRIVILEGED REBUKE

EARNING THE RIGHT TO SPEAK TO WHAT MATTERS

In the same way that every person has specific strengths and weaknesses, every church excels and fails in unique ways. Communities assume identities and create powerful cultural norms over time. Some of the elements of a church body's fundamental makeup are an asset while others become a liability. This is true for every community, every church.

If you land at a church that is somewhere other than where you grew up, these unique cultural identifiers will be easier to spot. Some may smack you in the face. To the extent that the local cultural distinctives are very different from your own community of origin, problematic norms will be more immediately obvious. And you will find yourself troubled.

As a shepherd committed to the health and well-being of the flock, you will want to get to work right away correcting these maladies. Because the issues are so obvious, you will feel particularly emboldened to address them with conviction. After all, you are a truth teller by trade.

And when you do speak out, the climate will sour. Your boldness, clarity, and passion will probably not translate into instant revival. Quite the opposite is likely. Newly minted shepherds quickly find themselves on the outs with the very people they have committed to serve. Rather than opening up, people are closing the pastor out. And feelings of rejection and isolation set in.

The immature shepherd might describe this experience as cross-bearing. But it is not. This is self-inflicted harm born out of a powerful combination of youthful pride and naivete. You are not in pain from the wounds of self-sacrificing love. You are in pain because you acted foolishly. Let me explain what likely went wrong.

Your initial assessments are superficial. You may have noticed right away that this community does not give generously to the church ministry. So you rightly addressed the matter. But you did not understand the long sordid history of church financial mis-management prior to your arrival. You may have noticed right away that this community does not engage with global missions. So you rightly brought correction. What you did not understand is that this group is deeply involved in local service, and the one overseas missionary sent from this church in the past decade is no longer walking with Christ.

I could point to many more examples of this mistake. But the root issue is an overconfidence in your initial assessments without the careful, patient work of growing in understanding. Through-out the sermon on the mount, Jesus repeated the prefacing phrase "You have heard it said." In doing so, he acknowledged that prior influences had powerfully shaped the way these people thought and acted.

When you speak out and preach your superficial assessments apart from relational understanding, everyone else realizes that you don't have a clue. People will pull away not because they are resistant to truth, but because they sense that you are uninterested in the hard work of getting to know them. They pull away because you are not acting lovingly.

You're not so perfect. In the same way that the sociocultural peculiarities of a new community are quickly evident to you, your own oddness is more obvious than you probably think. As quickly as you have pegged this group's specific issues, they have pegged yours. If you decide to immediately focus on treating their issues, do not be shocked when they get to work seeking a remedy for yours. If you are hasty to create a dynamic of critique, you will likely reap the fruit in kind.

Not all truth is for telling. Shepherds who feel a congregation putting up resistance against their critiques are often quick with this line of defense: "I only said those things because they are true." And yet the Scriptures are full of guidelines for knowing when to keep quiet.[1] Many things that are true should not be said. Many other things that are true should be said only to a certain audience. Still other things that are true should not be said until the right time.

Honesty can be a disguise for mean-spiritedness and relational laziness. "I don't want to do the work of making an appeal, so I'll just speak my mind."

Rebuke and correction are the privilege of relational capital, a return on investment. And like all investments, relational capital is built slowly over time. How do you know when it is time to speak directly to hard issues? I would suggest the following prerequisites: 1) You have developed a love for your people and your people know they are loved. 2) You understand underlying causes and historical factors contributing to systemic issues. 3) You are prepared to go beyond defining the problem by leading your people on the pathway of healing and freedom, speaking truth in an abundance of grace.

When correction is handled with maturity and humility, truth and grace, it will only increase your influence. People know when they are cared for even when the message is hard to hear. You will endear them to you by gently calling them into conformity with the image of Christ.

As time goes by, and you develop a stable reputation as a safe and skillful shepherd with confidence to engage difficult matters, a new kind of ministry opportunity will open up. Secret doors will open and you will be invited to speak truth and grace into deep

---

1. Prov 10:19; 11:12; 12:16, 23; 17:14, 27–28; 21:23

tragedies, generational sins, fragmented family groups. Only the most adept and sure-handed surgeons are given these invitations.

Here is a word of caution for preachers in small communities. Many of the stories you hear through your ministry of shepherding should not be used as illustrations in next weeks sermon. There are hundreds of stories I could have used in the writing of this book that I chose not to. Why? Because they are not my stories. If we are flippant or overly enthusiastic in the retelling of these stories, our people will grow more cautious about what they share. We all want powerful sermon illustrations! But if we are not careful, we will do more harm than good.

Think about how very few people know the most intimate details of your personal struggles and challenges. There is nothing we protect more carefully than the deep wounds of our own sinful brokenness. If you try to barge into this territory or behave recklessly once there, you will be locked out. If you faithfully love and serve your flock with gentleness and grace, you will be invited in. And your ministry of delivering the captives will take on new depth and power.

FOUNDATIONS
Part Two

Chapter 16

JOY

THE INVISIBLE FOUNTAIN

I remember driving past the business office of some old friends, noticing the vehicles of the husband and wife duo parked in the front and swinging in for a very belated catchup. It had been close to a year since we had last talked at any length. This couple does not attend my church or any church in town but they are good friends with some knowledge of God.

I wasn't prepared for the emotional intensity I blindly walked into. These two are business owners who are very tuned into the national political scene. The day I dropped in was just a couple of days after their party of choice had been defeated in the election. They were beside themselves. And I don't mean mad; I mean they were overwhelmed with anxiety about the future.

This kind of conversation is not new to anyone who spends any amount of time with other humans and I have had many. So, I pulled up a chair and heard their deep angst. Some of the concerns seemed far-fetched and some seemed entirely legitimate. I wasn't there to offer any answers really. My role is to show love to anxious angry people.

About thirty minutes into this conversation, the husband, who was choking back tears at this point, flatly posed a question. He wasn't accusatory or curious as much as he was maybe confused. "So, you're fine with all of this?" He was not asking about my political point of view. It was a somewhat bewildered acknowledgment that my presenting emotion wasn't matching up with their anger and angst.

"No, I am not fine with all of this. I think there are going to be some very difficult realities down the road as a result of all of this. However, I believe that God is still in control and will still bring about his intended outcomes, even if the path our country chooses is a painful one."

Silence.

If you are a pastor reading this, you know what it is like to sense when smart people think you are naive. Not in a judgmental or condescending way. They just know that you are very busy doing God's work and are clearly out of touch with the actual world they live in. They know that your smile and warmth are born out of ignorance and simplemindedness. What they don't know is that you have a front-row seat to human depravity in a way they would never likely imagine. My smile and warmth flow from a hidden source.

The Scriptures suggest that the Christians experience of peace beyond understanding, joy overflowing, and contentment in the face of suffering is the product not of external realities but of an internal one, not of external changes but of an internal one, not of environmental adjustments but of the transformation of my heart and mind. True joy is Christ in me, the hope of glory.[1]

When I am possessed by one desire that is, by many orders of magnitude, greater than all other desires, when I am able at all times to lay hold of and possess the object of that desire, and the object of my desire is profoundly and supremely satisfying; would this not impact the way others experience me? Especially those most intimately acquainted with me?

Would I not appear to be someone with a great and powerful inner satisfaction? And would not others note that even when bothered by other difficulties, this satisfaction, this contentment, this fullness would be observably stable?

---

1. Col 1:27.

The joy set before Jesus is the joy of relationship. He was after you and me. And he has me and I have him. The invitation to cross-bearing is the invitation to add to his joy and mine by bringing others into this relationship. I am not joyful and content because I am blindly ignorant of the world's brokenness. I am joyful and content because I am receiving that joy and peace from the only true source. And he has invited me to walk with him, as a cross-bearer, into a greater experience of this joy.

What do you point to as the explanation for your lack of peace? What do you point to as the explanation for your inability to experience joy in everything? What do you point to as the explanation for your lack of contentment, your inability to suffer with grace?

My confession is that when others around me have observed me as joyless, as discontent, as anxious, as dissatisfied, I have pointed the finger at many other explanations that draw attention away from my tepid love for and pursuit of Jesus. When he is not enough, nothing is ever enough.

> You will make known to me the path of life;
> In Your presence is fullness of joy;
> In Your right hand there are pleasures forever.[2]

Maximum joy, permanent joy.

> But whatever things were gain to me, those things I have counted as loss for the sake of Christ. More than that, I count all things to be loss in view of the surpassing value of knowing Christ Jesus my Lord, for whom I have suffered the loss of all things, and count them but rubbish so that I may gain Christ.[3]

All of the lesser sources of joy, many of which *can* be obtained, are as garbage. So vast is the disparity between the greater joy and these lesser joys, Paul gladly forfeits them all.

The joy of political victory and the peace derived from political power are rubbish when compared to the inestimable value

2. Ps 16:11.
3. Phil 3:7–8.

of knowing and being known by Jesus. And I know him and he knows me. Even if all of my dreams came true, they would not produce in me a joy like the joy that Jesus gives.

So don't be offended if I don't wring my hands. I will choose instead to lift them in praise. He is my joy. He is my peace. And his peace is perfect.

Chapter 17

RIGHTEOUSNESS

THE QUALIFYING ROLE OF OBEDIENCE

My own definition of human-made religion would be something like "All of the mechanisms and methods by which we encourage the greater power to act on our behalf." Religion is the earnest effort to please God(s) in order to compel God to do the things we want and to prevent the things we don't want. Misunderstood religion devolves into a transactional script for gaining the favor of the divine. "If you do this, God will do this."

Christianity has not been spared this very human tendency. I have been guilty of this very human tendency. I go to church, I give my money, I read my Bible, I pray at dinner, I do good things and avoid bad things, so that God will be more inclined to grant my desires. It is this mindset that causes most of us to ask "God, what I am doing wrong?" every time things do not go according to plan. If God is not doing what I wanted him to do, it must be that I missed an ingredient in the recipe I call religion. To fix the shortfall, I just need to add the missing piece.

For the religious person who believes that he or she is not doing Christianity very well, fear is constant and pervasive. I know what I should be doing, but I'm just not getting it done. Because I believe that God requires these things at which I am failing, it will come as no surprise when God drops the hammer. When something bad finally happens, I sadly acknowledge "Yep, I deserve this."

A religious Jesus would have prayed in Gethsemane, "God, what did I do to deserve this? Tell me where I went wrong, and I will repent."

Man-made religion is self-serving. For all the outward acts of benevolence and moral cleanliness, it ends up corrupted. The Pharisees manifested this corrupt expression of religion perfectly. And those who buy this message are not drawn to cross-bearing and the self-sacrifice it requires.

This is a plain truth of the ministry of Jesus; it was the righteousness of Jesus that qualified him for the ministry of cross-bearing.[1] The worst possible outcome of his ministry career was made possible by his perfect track record.[2] It was because he had no sin of his own that he was able to take the weight of our sin upon his shoulders and die on our behalf.

It is through the transforming miracle of the gospel that we are freed from self-pursuit to truly love others.[3] A loving person, a truly good person, when suffering hostility or hardship, does not turn to God and say, "I don't deserve this!" If you believe that being good precludes you from cross-bearing, you don't understand goodness as God defines it. A loving person comes to God and says, "Not my will but yours be done." If God says this is the loving way, the loving person is fully committed without remorse.

Is this not a basic truth laid out through the life of Job? It was his righteous credentials that caught the attention of God and gave God confidence that Job was capable of fulfilling an incredibly difficult assignment. Job certainly asked, "Why, God?" His religious friends made it clear that God only allows the wicked to carry

---

1. 2 Cor 5:21: "He made Him who knew no sin to be sin in our behalf, so that we might become the righteousness of God in Him."

2. 1 John 3:5: "You know that He appeared in order to take away sins; and in Him there is no sin."

3. Gal 5:13–14: "For you were called to freedom, brothers [and sisters;] only do not turn your freedom into an opportunity for the flesh, but serve one another through love. For the whole Law is fulfilled in one word, in the statement, 'You shall love your neighbor as yourself.'"

crosses. But their religious reasoning was wrong. Job's unparalleled commitment to God qualified him for the suffering he endured.

If a shepherd is inclined toward religiosity, he may believe that through moral goodness, the favor of God can be purchased in the form of material benefits. "If I am a good pastor and behave well and serve others, God will bless me with a growing, stable, financially sound ministry full of mature people pleading to volunteer." When ministry inevitably runs into the quagmire of human adversity this pastor asks "God why?! I was being good."

After asking why, this misguided leader slips into the biggest mistake of all, "God, what lesson do you want me to learn from this?" Which is the Christian way of asking God "What did I fail to give you that you now require in order to make the suffering stop? Whatever it is, tell me now and I'll learn the lesson quickly!" This is transactionalism. Crosses are for slow learners so I'll learn quickly and skip the suffering.

But should we not want to learn lessons from suffering? Yes, we should want to learn lessons from suffering. The first lesson we should want to learn is how to suffer well. But this is not the lesson I described above. The lesson that the immature follower wants to learn is the lesson of how not to suffer. The problem with this thinking is that cross-bearing is not a lesson, it is the whole ministry. God gave you this cup for a purpose far beyond you.

The shepherd obsessed with ending his or her suffering is the shepherd who wants something other than the shepherding ministry. And this gets to the heart of pastoral burnout and disillusionment. It is not because it is too difficult, it is because the suffering is so surprising, coming in ways so unexpected. These leaders do not yet understand the ministry of cross-bearing as it is worked out in the role of the shepherd. "God, take this cup from me. My will be done, or I can't do this anymore." I've been there myself.

All obedience to God can be summed up in one command: love.[4] And love is explained to us with a cross. If righteousness

---

4. Matt 22:37–40: "And He said to him, 'You shall love the lord your god with all your heart, and with all your soul, and with all your mind.' This is the great and foremost commandment. The second is like it, 'You shall love your

is best understood as love and love is best understood as cross-bearing, this explains why cross-bearing is only attractive to the righteous. To suggest that righteousness should preclude cross-bearing is to suggest that love should eliminate loving.

The righteousness of Jesus was not only his qualifier, it was his motivator. Because he was righteous, he was able to save. Because he was righteous, he *wanted* to save.

The pressure on the shepherd to always do the *right* thing because righteousness requires it, is replaced by a sincere desire to do the *loving* thing because love desires it. The burden of righteousness does not transform my inner person. Only the love of my cross-bearing Savior can do that.

Stop telling yourself you *have* to be loving. You are invited by God and enabled by God to love and receive love from him and others.

Stop telling yourself you *have* to have a pristine marriage. You are invited by God and enabled by God to love your spouse. This is righteousness.

Stop telling yourself you *have* to have model children. You are invited by God and enabled by God to love your children. This is righteousness.

Stop telling yourself you *have* to have an enviable church. You are invited by God and enabled by God to love your flock. This is righteousness.

Unconditional self-sacrificing love for God and others is all of righteousness. There is no shame in it. There is great joy and eternal glory! This is cross-bearing ministry. When your heart believes this is true, a fundamental motivational transformation begins to take place.

Now, let's take this a step further.

---

neighbor as yourself.' Upon these two commandments hang the whole Law and the Prophets."

Chapter 18

AGAPE

THE RELATIONSHIP OF LOVE AND SUFFERING

It is the fundamental need of every human that has ever existed, from birth to the grave. It is both the greatest commandment and summary commandment; love God and love your neighbor. We are made to give and receive love. It is that which undergirds and supports every other aspect of our human purpose. Love ensures human flourishing. Yes, go to work; yes, improve the world; yes, raise a family; yes, build a community, and all through love.

The Scriptures describe different kinds of love. There is the affectionate love of family, the comradery of friendship, and the sensual love of romance. The highest form of love is agape or divine love. It is love characterized by unconditional self-sacrifice in pursuit of another's good. Agape love elevates each of the other kinds of love. It is this love that John speaks of in his letters to the church.

> Beloved, let's love one another; for love is from God, and everyone who loves has been born of God and knows God. The one who does not love does not know God, because God is love. By this the love of God was revealed in us, that God has sent his only Son into the world so that we may live through him. In this is love, not that we loved God, but that He loved us and sent his Son to be a sacrifice for our sins. Beloved, if God so loved us, we also

ought to love one another. . . . We love, because He first loved us.[1]

According to one of Christ's closest friends, God is love. It is his fundamental nature. Furthermore, all love has its origin with God and is sustained by and through God. In order that we might understand this love, God has perfectly demonstrated it to us and for us through Jesus and his cross.

And here is a great paradox. The cross is what we look to in order to understand love as God defines it and yet the cross is a picture of an intense, even grotesque level of suffering. This is one of the deeper mysteries of the cross and the nature of its message regarding God's love.

If the cross was God's plan from the foundation of the world, then suffering was God's plan from the foundation of the world.

The tree of the knowledge of good and evil, planted in the garden, would lead to the human experience of love and suffering. For too long, I only understood suffering as fundamental to the problem.

Do you remember Peter's words? "But if when you do what is right and suffer for it you patiently endure it, this finds favor with God. For you have been called for this purpose, because Christ also suffered for you, leaving you an example, *so that you would follow in His steps.*"[2]

The cross was not only Christ's purpose, it perfectly illustrates and explains our purpose and ensures us that in fulfilling our purpose we discover the favor of God. This is the same God who chose the cross from before the world began because it was the pathway to the greatest joy. If the cross is God's instruction manual for love, then love and suffering are connected. The message of the cross as the prototype for love says that suffering is fundamental to the solution, it is fundamental to achieving the desired outcome.

My confession is that I want to be loved, and I would be willing to love, if receiving love could be somewhat assured and the

1. 1 John 4:4–11, 19.

2. 1 Pet 2:20b–2.1

cost of love could be kept to a tolerable limit. I like the idea of love, not of suffering. But this is not agape love.

Agape love is unconditional self-sacrifice in pursuit of another's good. In order to learn and experience this love I must have a choice and conditions! There must be real and painful conditions that I freely choose not to make my conditions of self-sacrifice.

The question is, will I pursue this person's good, at great cost to myself, given certain painful conditions? Unconditional love, by definition, is on the other side of my response to those conditions. My experience of this kind of love is not diminished by the assault against its existence, it is by very definition increased.

A person who was formerly friendly has become hostile. I love this person and want to continue to pursue their good. If I decide to continue loving this person, it is going to cost me. They are going to say and do harmful things. But I decide the harm this person causes will not become a condition of my commitment to show love. This decision, which involves suffering, has elevated my love for this person to the level of agape love.

Suffering enlarges, enriches, and empowers my experience of love.

Agape love is born out of suffering. Suffering is agape's necessary prerequisite. Jesus himself "learned obedience through what He suffered."[3] What is obedience? Love! Jesus learned agape love through the suffering he endured. He chose not to make our sin a condition of his love, and in that choice, agape love was perfected in him.

According to human wisdom, the cross is the death of love, but the cross, according to divine wisdom is love's doorway. If I only understand suffering as inherent to the problem, my view is incomplete. The cross teaches us that suffering is inherent to the solution, that suffering is the pathway to joy because suffering enlarges, enriches, and empowers our experience of love.

Jesus loved them until the end.[4] The end being proof that he ever loved at all. And here is my honest and painful confession:

3. Heb 5:8.

4. John 13:1.

much of what I have called love falls far short of the unconditional self-sacrificing love of God. Why? I change my mind when I suffer. I love until it hurts too much.

There seems to be two basic human responses to suffering; radical control or radical detachment. In order to mitigate the cost of suffering, my natural disposition is to choose one or the other. I use control in order to prevent or reduce suffering or I detach myself from my experience of suffering. I personally gravitate toward detachment.

But the ugly truth, whether in the home, in the church, or in our community, is that efforts toward radical control or radical detachment always increase human suffering. Furthermore, radical control eliminates the possibility of love while radical detachment disables my experience of love.

And there stands the cross. Jesus chose not to fight back. He chose not to run away. He submitted to his Father with an eye toward our benefit, and with a resolve to pay whatever price love required. He laid down his life, he loved them until the end. "I am the good shepherd; the good shepherd lays down His life for the sheep."[5] And through the suffering of the cross, his love was made perfect.

The invitation to you, in whatever suffering you currently face, is to entrust yourself to the God who is love so he can lead you into a greater experience of his great gift of Love.

Take up your cross, for joy, for love, for righteousness, for fellowship with Your Savior. Do not hold back now. It is time to go all in.

5. John 10:11.

Chapter 19

JUSTICE

RESTORING REAL POWER TO THE POWERLESS

When improperly understood, a directive to take up your cross can become authoritarian abuse. I have sat with many victims during my time in ministry, men and women who have been abused in every way at every age. I have heard agonizing stories of infidelity, indiscretion, injustice, felony assault, embezzlement, and trauma of all kinds.

But there is one storyline that is so shocking, each time I hear it told I find myself fighting the natural urge to physically recoil. There are many versions of this story but one familiar plotline: An abused person works up the courage to share their ongoing experience with a spiritual authority only to be sent back into the abusive situation.

Why would a shepherd send an abused person back into an abusive situation? Because of a fundamental and dangerous misunderstanding of cross-bearing.

Cross-bearing is the call of every believer. Yet as discussed in chapter 3, not all opportunities to suffer can be or should be accepted. Jesus and Paul showed us that sometimes we must get away rather than go along. There is a kind of hostility and harm that is not part of God's redemptive purpose and we are to flee from it. And the decision to get away or go along is one that I must make in prayerful conversation with God. *Take up your cross and follow Me.*

In your ministry, you will come across victims of harm who do not have a viable getaway option, perhaps for financial reasons, psychological reasons like fear or uncertainty or stress from trauma. But there is a kind of person who is suffering and cannot, in his or her own power, choose to get away. This person is shackled and chained and does not hold the key.

This was not the situation that Jesus faced. Jesus had two viable options that the Father afforded him; get away or go along. The getaway option was one that the Father was willing to facilitate. It was important to the Father and the Son that the Son make the decision to take up his cross as a free expression of his own choice. There was no coercion. "Or do you think that I cannot appeal to My Father, and He will at once put at My disposal more than twelve legions of angels?"[1] The Father did not facilitate the victimization of the Son. Jesus knew the Father was standing at the ready, willing to intervene, willing to support the getaway option.

Biblical justice means to intervene in situations of harm and hostility to ensure that victims are granted two viable options, get away or go along. It requires me to ensure that the getaway option is fully available to this person who does not have the power to ensure that option for himself or herself. A victim is powerless. Justice restores the person's power without diminishing it in other ways.

For a shepherd to assume the getaway or go-along decision on the part of the harmed individual is to take on the role of the Holy Spirit and do what the Father was unwilling to do for the Son; make the decision for him. This person needs to follow Jesus and hear from him about his will. My role is to ensure that this person is not powerless in that decision. I do this by adding what power I have to the getaway option.

Only get away. The shepherd who assumes too much authority in matters of justice will not allow autonomy of choice to the person being harmed. We covered this already, but this is the same

1. Matt 26:53.

mistake Peter made. To tell a person that to get away is the only option is to diminish their independence and ignore their redemptive calling. "I've decided based on my assessment that I will not let you consider going along." By doing this, I overrule their personhood.

There are rare instances in which a person is so traumatized by a harmful situation that they simply do not have the capacity to make decisions about that situation until they are removed from it. Because this individual cannot make a getaway or go-along decision, I step in and remove the person from the situation until he or she is able to fully own the decision. Is this not what Jesus did for us? Unable to rescue ourselves from the bondage of evil, he intervened and set us free to choose love.[2] In doing so, he did not usurp my humanity, he honored my humanity by liberating me.

Children fall into this category. Often unable to make sophisticated decisions about their own redemptive calling in the face of hostility or harm, I do what is required by law and conscience to ensure that they are removed from these situations. In lower-stakes situations, like a condescending or manipulative peer relationship, I encourage my own kids to follow Christ in their own uncoerced cross-bearing decisions while making myself fully available to intervene. "Do you think that I cannot appeal to my Dad?"

Only go along. The shepherd who sends the harmed person back into a harmful situation is also usurping the victim's humanity but toward a more destructive outcome. To refuse this person a legitimate getaway or go along option is to partner with the abuser and revictimize the abused. The calling of cross-bearing is not something that can be forced upon another person. This is not the way of Jesus. To force someone into cross-bearing is to become the crucifier. God will forgive you, but what you are doing is wrong.

"I broke the jaws of the wicked and rescued the prey from his teeth."[3] Job, the most righteous man of his time, knew when to step in and rescue. He would not be complacent when evil jaws crushed unwilling prey. And God honored his commitment.

2. Col 1:13: "For He rescued us from the domain of darkness, and transferred us to the kingdom of His beloved Son."

3. Job 29:17.

Justice restores a person's power without diminishing it in other ways.

What do we already know? It is so important that a cross-bearer hears from God on the question of whether to go along or get away. And in many situations, the word of God has already spoken on the specifics. There will be instances when a person wants a shepherd to intervene in matters of "injustice" in a way contrary to the revealed will of God.

No matter how deeply offended you may be, I cannot negate the "turn the other cheek"[4] principles of Scripture in my response to your situation. Although your marriage may be disappointing and your spouse may be treating you unfairly, I will not ignore the abundance of biblical discussion on marriage in order to partner more fully with the idea of your victimization. If the Scripture speaks on an issue, start there. After considering the revealed will of God, seek his personal will for you in your decision to get away or go along.

Can you do what I will not do? Although this has been a rare experience in my ministry, there are those who will hyperbolize their situation in an effort to rouse my sympathies and manipulate my involvement. They are attempting to dispense of their free choice and coerce me into a position where I feel obligated to make cross-bearing decisions on their behalf. Rather than making careful choices and owning those choices, they cling to their own victimization and cry out for help. They pray, "Father, my will be done. But can you do it for me?"

Matters of injustice can feel like a minefield for the inexperienced shepherd. They will require prayer, greater discernment, and carefully selected mentors who can help you navigate these complex scenarios with an eye toward cross-bearing.

But fear not. Jesus will lead you as you follow him.

---

4. Matt 5:38–42.

Chapter 20

INITIATIVE

INTENTIONALITY IN CROSS-BEARING

As a bright-eyed teen I was not one for taking big risks, especially social risks. Later in life I learned the benefit of trying things that might fail, but as a young high-school student, I preferred to blend in and not stand out. But this fear came with its setbacks.

Our school had numerous banquets throughout the year and during my first two years in high school, I never invited a girl to one. My junior year, much to my relief, I was invited to a Sadie Hawkins banquet by the girl to whom I have now been married for the past twenty-five years. I'm glad my wife showed some risk-taking initiative all those years ago. It really worked out in my favor!

As an adult, I occasionally bump into remnants of those same fears from long ago. I find myself avoiding conversations with people I think might dislike me, carry resentment toward me or even bear hostility toward me. I may avoid opportunities to interact with those who show gross immaturities or aggressive tendencies. I don't like the feeling of rejection, so I am prone to test the waters of acceptance before jumping into the pool.

While there are some self-serving benefits of these tendencies, there is also one major problem; it's not the way that God relates.

We love God because God took the initiative to love us when we were not yet receptive to his outreach. He was not motivated by a guilty sense of obligation to us. He was motivated by the joy set before Him. And so, he left heaven along with His divine privileges and came to us to serve us by dying for us.[1]

We love because He first loved us.[2]

Once I understand the purposes of God in cross-bearing, once I understand it as my calling, for the joy set before me, I simply cannot passively stand by and wait for an opportunity to come knocking at my door. Jesus did not wait for us to come pounding on the door of heaven, pleading for his help. He demonstrates his love for us in this way, while we were still hostile, he came and died for us.[3] Before we knew our need, before we were willing to ask for our salvation, he provided it at great cost to himself.

When I avoid cross-bearing I reveal an inner conviction that the pain of it isn't worth the joy of it. I do not scorn the shame of it, I agree with the shame of it. The joy of it is too hypothetical and distant to get me beyond my natural instincts. I prefer to blend in and not stand out. Not because I am unwilling to help—I just know that it might go poorly. Because they are not asking, I am not offering. And I console myself regarding my passivity by assuring myself that if someone knocked on my door I would open. Of course, I would!

But I didn't knock on God's door. He knocked on mine.[4] He first loved me and came to me in my need.

As a cross-bearing shepherd I have grown in this commitment; I refuse to allow the potential for harm to prevent me from pursuing joy. I realize that when I step in to offer a helping hand, I may be misunderstood, I may be rejected, I may be betrayed. But

1. Phil 2:5–8.

2. 1 John 4:19.

3. Rom 5:8: "But God demonstrates His own love toward us, in that while we were still sinners, Christ died for us."

4. Rev 3:20: "Behold, I stand at the door and knock; if anyone hears My voice and opens the door, I will come in to him and will dine with him, and he with Me."

that is up to God. I cannot walk away from so much potential. I do not wait for these opportunities, I find them.

Plenty of good people are willing to do the right thing. The very term "right thing" speaks of necessity, duty, obligation. Do it because it is *right*! But cross-bearing isn't just the right thing to do, it is the infinitely more valuable thing to do. It will lead to an indescribably consequential reward that I will enjoy for all eternity. Jesus didn't come because it was the right thing; he came because it was the best thing, the greater thing, the thing that leads to the most joy.

To love like Jesus is to take the initiative in loving before reciprocation is assured. Jesus, at the last supper, realizing the Father had given him everything, responded by taking the initiative to serve his betrayer and his deserters.[5] One final opportunity to love his own.

As an initiative-taking cross-bearer, it will be important to revisit the concepts in chapter 3 regarding timing. I cannot jump at every opportunity to forfeit my life; I am not the savior of the world, and my resources are limited. But to say that I cannot accept every opportunity is to acknowledge that while cross-bearing is a mode of operation that encompasses all of my life, there are many more opportunities than I can reasonably pursue. I can maintain an initiative-taking posture at all times while not pursuing all opportunities.

There are a couple of initiative-taking opportunities that should be automatic; in these relationships I am always leading the charge. In these relationships I never wait to be asked, I am vigilant to maintain a proactive posture. First in my marriage. Then in my role as a father. For this small group that I call my family, I must leap at opportunities to lay down my life motivated by love. If no one else in my household is feeling it, sign me up, I am ready to go. I will not be passive.

5. John 13:3–4: "Jesus, knowing that the Father had handed all things over to him, and that He had come forth from God and was going back to God, got up from supper and laid His outer garments [aside;] and He took a towel and tied it around himself."

There are many cross-bearing opportunities. Opportunities for self-sacrificing service are too many to count. Some people will come knocking on your door. But many will not. Some people will hide in the shadows, suffering silently, alone and afraid. Some people will lash out the moment you reach out your caring hands. In some cases, you should take the initiative and go to them anyway. Take up your cross and follow him.

PRACTICUM
The Pastor

Chapter 21

YOUR IDEALISM

DESTRUCTIVE WISHFUL THINKING

Two Bible college students decided to get serious about seeking God in prayer. They began praying together every morning before class. Soon, other students joined them for prayer and the prayer group expanded to include other schools. Eventually this prayer movement became a mission movement that spanned the globe.

A young pastor was presenting his congregation with the need for a new building space for Sunday services. The young congregation was growing and expanding and the dilapidated structure they called their church had fallen into a desperate level of disrepair. As he shared the need with his congregation, one of his elders stood up and convincingly challenged his church to meet the need "right now." By the time the service was over, they had raised $200,000, a down payment on a new building.

A local church invited an itinerant speaker to do evening services for one week. After the first night of speaking, there was a strong sense that the Spirit of God was moving. People ended up staying for several hours to pray and worship together. The crowd grew over the week and several dozen people were saved. The final service lasted four hours as people repented and recommitted to Christ.

I have heard some version of each of these stories over the years, told by a pastor. I have heard many other stories with similar qualities. I think the intent is to paint a grand picture of what is possible when we submit our lives fully to God. These stories are meant to inspire the listener. But they often do just the opposite.

Is there anything wrong with sharing testimonies of God's faithfulness? Of course not. In fact, it is necessary to the health of a church to hear such stories. So, what is the problem?

Pastoral storytelling tends to focus on what delights the pastor. If the testimonies he chooses are usually stories of how God has moved in the lives of his people, it communicates that he finds great joy through God's work in his flock. But if the stories he tells are *always* extreme, once-in-a-lifetime types of events (e.g., formation of a mission's movement), it may mean he is frustrated by the mundane work of shepherding hearts. And if the testimonies he chooses are always stories about what God is doing somewhere else, it may mean that he wishes his church was more like some other church, or that these Christians were more like some other Christians.

Imagine if I did this to my wife. In an effort to encourage her growth as a wife and mother, I come home everyday armed with new stories about how someone else's wife is setting the example. I am going to be very effective in convincing her that I really wish I was married to someone else.

Lamenting your flock's inability to attain to your lofty visions for them is not cross-bearing. God delights in his people.[1] The bride of Christ is the bride of his joyful choosing. However, suffering constant comparisons that reflect a discontented heart will become their cross to bear.

This is not an issue of gifting fit. This is a form of idealism characteristic of immaturity. Do you find your highest joy through the fellowship of cross-bearing as you follow in the footsteps of Jesus? Or do you often wish for some dramatic spectacle? Do you believe you would be a happier pastor if your people were more

---

1. Psa 149:4: "For the LORD takes pleasure in His people; He will glorify the lowly with salvation."

impressive? Do you gaze at glossy reports of other ministries and wish your ministry was more like theirs? Don't forget, a peaceable and quiet life is something to be commended, something God smiles upon.[2]

At some point you need to come to terms with two realities. First, your unhappiness is your issue and no church, no matter how great, will fix it. Second, your idealism is harmful to the healthy growth of your flock. Constant comparison will not motivate the ministry growth you desire.

To mature, you must deny yourself. Deny your wishful thinking. You must cease your efforts to force people in line with your idealistic vision. You must apply all that effort toward bringing your own heart in line with God's vision. And what is God's vision? "And God demonstrates His own love in this way, while we were still sinners, Christ died for us."[3] He loved and served you while you were disappointing him.

Today, that means serving my still-sinning flock, with self-sacrificing love, for the joy set before me.

2. 1 Tim 2:2b–3: "So that we may lead a tranquil and quiet life in all godliness and dignity. This is good and acceptable in the sight of God our Savior."
3. Rom 5:8.

Chapter 22

THEIR IDEALISM

THE WOUNDS OF CONSTANT COMPARISON

When my children first entered the school-age years, I spectated at a lot of lousy events. Jenny and I have watched soccer matches, musicals, swim meets, track meets, ballets, and piano recitals to name a few. They all had one thing in common; they weren't very good. I could have found better sports, better music, better production value pretty much anywhere else. But I was not in attendance to witness greatness, I was in attendance to see my own kids. My kids were adorable.

I pastor in a small Alaskan community, a town of about 6,000 people. If you go twenty miles in every direction you might be able to scoop up another 4,000 people. We are not a big church. Our production value is consistent with our church size. And if you want something better, you could watch just about anything you find online. We will never compete on that level.

For the most part, people get it. In fact, many who live in small communities prefer smaller church gatherings because they are more consistent with our lifestyle. But both those who appreciate it for what it is and those who wish it was something more will eventually share their comparative critiques. "I was at this one church and I really liked the way they handled communion." Or "I was watching this service online and they included video testimonies as part of their service." This is all good information.

Some people will not spare you from a litany of comparisons. They seem unaware of the demoralizing impact and don't seem to consider that the pace at which they offer suggestions would be unrealistic even if I decided to implement every single one of them. But I find that these people are easy to deflect. I understand they may not intend to do harm or be aware of how they come across and I give myself permission to hold their constant critiques loosely.

The more difficult burden is the sum total of critiques offered by the people you trust, want to hear from, and truly value. They do not offer constant critiques. Their critiques and comparisons are only occasional and usually have some weight. But when a few hundred well-meaning people offer an occasional comparison, it can add up to become a heavy burden. You will have days where the stars align and you receive several back-to-back comparisons to other ministries doing something better than you are. No one collaborated to pile it up that way, but even if they are worth considering, you will lay a heavy head on your pillow that night.

An additional tension created by your members' critiques is the double-binding effect of comparisons. A double-bind is two forces pulling in the opposite direction that make it impossible to move. In ministry, you will be measured against the most-gifted and famous leaders in the land. And when a famous gifted pastor stumbles into immorality and collapses, somehow you will feel implicated as a fellow minister. It is a weird experience. The same person who suggested we be more like church X is now very casually denouncing the culture of that same church in the context of broader but vague critiques of American church culture.

The message seems to be, can you make our church more like all of the other churches that are doing things better while avoiding all of the things that make those churches problematic?

This double-bind will start to feel like a cross over time. You will hear stories of the pastor who is known for being available *every* time anyone calls his personal cell. And stories about the pastor who is known for giving his undivided, uninterrupted attention when sitting down to talk. But you can't be both.

As a shepherd you are always failing someone's expectations. Even your closest allies have at least one or two expectations that you will never meet. Remember, cross-bearing is first about what God is doing in you. There is a divine role these critiques are to play in your life as a shepherd.

First, these hard-to-hear opinions are meant to strengthen and mature your dependence upon the will of the Father. "Blessed are those who are not offended by me."[1] Jesus knew the weight of others' expectations. And he repeatedly doubled down on his commitment to obey his Father. If you commit to following the Father's will and the Son's example, some good people aren't going to like the specific way you are doing it. And this is okay. Do not long lament the death of your own ego. The subtle barbs provide an opportunity to address your heart. Take up your cross, and scorn its shame.

Some people solve this dilemma by proudly declaring "I don't care about the opinions of others anymore!" This only reflects failure on the second lesson God is trying to teach you. A Shepherd must learn to love and serve those who wound the ego, not simply tolerate or ignore them. If I choose not to care anymore, I must become numb or calloused. I must rid myself of a tender heart, something God says he desires.[2]

I do care what my people think. But I have decided that I will not be controlled by what they think even as I carefully consider what they think. There is always some truth to be gleaned if I am humble enough and secure enough to keep listening.

Daunting? It can be. But the cross calls us to an unwavering commitment to serve the needs of others while refusing to be deterred by the wounds they cause.

---

1. Matt 11:6.

2. Ezek 36:26: "Moreover, I will give you a new heart and put a new spirit within you; and I will remove the heart of stone from your flesh and give you a heart of flesh."

And here again is the trap that ensnares immature shepherds, the search for pity. Don't satisfy your wounded ego with the salve of another person's honey sweet sympathies. "I can't believe anyone would say such a thing to such a wonderful leader like you!" These comments often appeal to my carnal nature. Instead of settling for a lesser reward, go to Jesus. He understands.

As you grow in him you will discover that as your capacity for love becomes more stable, it leads to a similarly stable joy.

Chapter 23

THEIR PESSIMISM
THE IMPACT OF PRIOR MINISTRY WOUNDS

During the first year of planting a church with a good friend of mine, I called up a local business owner who had been attending. This business owner was very successful and close in age to my parents. "Hey, I was wondering if you would have time in your schedule to connect sometime in the next couple of weeks." I was excited to develop this friendship. But the response caught me by surprise; "Sure." Brief pause. "Am I in trouble for something?"

Every person that walks in the door of your church has wounds from previous relationships and experiences. And some of those who walk through your doors with a prior church background have a particular kind of wound; ministry leadership wounds. Some of these wounded people understand their wounds and some do not. Some have found healing for these wounds and some have not.

Hearing stories of ministry leadership wounds is easily one of the most troubling aspects of the shepherding ministry. At some level, because of my own role, I feel a deep sense of personal responsibility. But it is true, many people have endured some really terrible things at the hands of those charged with their spiritual care. And these wounds deeply affect the way these people relate to you, their pastor. There is a reason a successful business leader assumes an unsolicited call from a young pastor means trouble.

Used and abused. Some people who have been hurt by ministry leaders manifest their wounds with expressions of guilt. From the very first time you meet, they will apologize repeatedly for not doing more. They may walk into your church beaten up and exhausted and yet deeply ashamed of their inability to dive into the deep end of ministry involvement. "I used to volunteer four days a week but I just don't have the energy for it right now. I am really sorry I am not able to do more."

The best balm for this person is much-needed rest and permission to seek it. "I want to give you my permission to not involve yourself in serving right now. It sounds like you need some respite and I want you to know it's okay. You are welcome to come and enjoy without pressure. When you are ready to get involved, let me know, but take your time." When you care for people first, you refuse to use them to the breaking point.

Keep to yourself. Another common ministry leadership wound is expressed through a person's expectations of punitive behavior. This individual has been trained by prior experiences to expect that disagreements always become personal issues and lead to punishing reactions. It is a strange experience when a new acquaintance seems to have you pegged as an easily offended, closed-minded, selfishly motivated pastor who despises dissent and quickly punishes those who express it. Although it is easy to feel defensive, acting defensively will only confirm the worst assumptions about you.

The best balm for this person is exposure to a new set of cultural norms. There is not a good way to confront these dark expectations head-on and direct efforts to do so will more than likely trigger an aggressive response. It is much like the dog that has been mistreated by a previous owner. No matter your kind intentions, they will likely nip at your hand for a while. This is a kind of hostility that you should endure if at all possible, as you seek to model a more loving way. Take up your cross, scorn the shame, and love like Jesus.

Please like me. Yet another common ministry leadership wound is expressed as an intense drive to be liked and valued by the pastor. Often this person will figure out who is in charge and be face to face with the lead pastor after their first or second visit. Although there is nothing inherently wrong with wanting to meet the pastor on day one, you will notice after a few weeks that this new parishioner is not interested in getting to know anyone else. He or she uses all the jargon of an insider and behaves as if your relationship is much more substantial than it is.

The best balm for this person is healthy boundaries. An immature leader may be tempted to receive this new attention as flattery. But this broken soul is not enamored of your abilities, they are enamored of the feeling they get from being tight with the person in charge. It is possible that he or she has previously served in environments where there was a massive authority disparity between the lead pastor and other leaders. If you wanted clout, it came only from the top dog. And sadly, when you establish boundaries consistent with the newness of your relationship, this kind of wounded believer may vanish as quickly as they appeared. If you will not feed their broken desire for validation, they will find it somewhere else.

Just as God is patient with us when we treat him like our fallen human parents, we can be patient when people treat us like a former shepherd. And there is no point in putting those former shepherds on trial. You can validate the pain of leadership wounds without assigning blame. It could be that the last pastor was a mean guy who hurt people. It could be that he was a mature guy with healthy boundaries that immature people found offensive and off-putting. You just don't know.

But it doesn't matter. God's grace is available for the wounds caused by others and the wounds of our own doing. We can extend grace to wounded people in the same way. Don't take it personally. Deny yourself, take up your cross.

Chapter 24

FADING GRACE

THE WORDS-OF-ENCOURAGEMENT WEANING PROCESS

I remember the excitement I felt when my oldest child took her first unassisted steps. One foot in front of another, two or three paces, before rolling onto the floor. Jenny and I cheered her on and applauded her advancing capabilities. We even bribed her to try it again. And she did. Every step led to another vocal outburst, "Look at you! You are walking by yourself! You are so big now!"

And then a funny thing happened. Some time went by, and we stopped celebrating her ability to walk on her own. In fact, she now walks and runs like a champ every day and I never so much as even acknowledge her bipedal abilities. I can't remember the last time I said, "Look at you walking!"

There is a necessary adjustment that happens in ministry over time. You may feel as if you went to bed Rachel and woke up Leah. And just in case you forgot, Leah was the plain-looking sister. It doesn't happen immediately but it does happen. And if you don't understand what is happening, you may be left to think that you've grown unattractive, unable to impress.

The abundance of verbal encouragement in your first ministry experiences is a better indicator of your inexperience than it is your ability. Try it some Sunday; put a stumbling, bumbling, barely articulate soul on stage to share a personal testimony. People will line up afterward to tell them what a great job they did. Why? Not because they did a great job, but because they did something difficult, something that was out of their wheelhouse. They will receive praise as a form of encouragement.

But put that same soul on stage for the next fifty-two weeks and the mood will change. Encouragement will wane. Grace fades for weaknesses that were initially endearing. Now, if you are going to be on stage, you do need to eventually be good at what you are doing. You need to bring the goods. But ministry gifts are like a baby learning to walk. We praise the newness of the experience, even though we all recognize that babies are actually pretty clumsy walkers.

Some will incorrectly describe this as the honeymoon phase. The honeymoon phase is the period of time where another person can do no wrong because I am blinded to that person's faults. That is not what I am describing here. The early abundance of grace and encouragement is not due to a blindness to your faults, it is encouragement offered in spite of your faults because the encouragers believe that your faults will eventually be overcome as you grow in experience. And as you get better at walking, fewer people will feel compelled to say "Look at you walking!"

This transition must happen. Early ministry experiences feel good primarily because of what I receive in response. I need the verbal encouragement in order to feel good about myself and my ministry abilities. And I feel good about my effort according to what I got, not necessarily as a direct correlation of what I gave. My experience of peace and joy is the effect of having my own self-esteem appetites fed.

Don't be too hard on yourself. We all wrestle through immaturity issues. With grace, deny yourself.

The natural and healthy progression of ministry maturation requires you to get better at what you do while growing accustomed to receiving less verbal encouragement for doing it. If you are effective in ministry, positive encouragement won't disappear, but it will become less frequent.

For the uninformed shepherd, this can become a source of discouragement and even resentment. The feeling of being underappreciated is a common theme with pastors. "I work so hard, and hardly anyone says thank you anymore." This sentiment might be translated "I purchased encouragement from these people by serving them, and they didn't pay their bill." A pastor may even resort to getting the same endorphin boost by checking out their social media performance. This is all a trap.

Weaning yourself from your powerful dependence on positive encouragement is not cross-bearing. Weaning is self-denial, a prerequisite to cross-bearing. If you insist on making it about you, you will hardly be qualified for the redemptive suffering of cross-bearing. It's time to grow up. Be a fountain of encouragement for others, even when there is only a trickle coming your way.

To the degree that people perceive you to be a stable, secure person, they will not feel obligated to drench you with compliments to keep you propped up. And in ministry, this is a win. Even if encouragement is rare, it will become more substantial. Substantive encouragement is meaningfully connected to the real effect you have on the lives of others. "This is how God spoke to me through your teaching . . ." As opposed to "Good job, pastor."

And just in case you are led to believe that I am suggesting that a shepherd should be delivered from any need for encouragement, let me offer this: Find encouragement from a small select group of people who know you deeply enough to see the good and the bad and who have the capacity to encourage you with substance and insight. Find encouragement from those who are not afraid to invite you to cross-bearing. Find your encouragement through true fellowship with those not prone to flattery. And know that Christ will be there to encourage you as well.

Chapter 25

PASTOR'S PARKING

THE NURTURE OF YOUR SELF-IMPORTANCE

It wasn't until a year or two ago that I realized that National Sibling Day was a thing. I saw a picture one of my siblings posted on social media with the caption "Happy Sibling Day!" I like my siblings a lot. But I'm not sure what the expectation is now that we have a day dedicated in their honor. I should mention now that I have twelve siblings. This could get out of hand.

Another important day I didn't know about until after beginning in ministry was Pastors Appreciation Day. My first experience with being appreciated on a Pastors Appreciation Day was nice. Some nice things were said, and some thoughtful gifts given. I felt seen and cared for.

The following year I was geared up for it. I was looking forward to being recognized and validated for my noble efforts. I was floating on air as I headed to church that Sunday morning. But that year wasn't quite like the previous year. I think someone else had been put in charge of appreciation efforts. It wasn't quite as grand. And I felt let down by my own newly developed expectations.

Pastoral perks are an odd animal in the context of cross-bearing.

I remember years ago attending a youth event at a church in another city. One of the guest speakers decided to pull into the

"Pastors Parking" spot to unload his gear through the entrance. When he returned to his car, he discovered the pastor had parked bumper to bumper, trapping his vehicle in the reserved parking spot. The pastor was nowhere to be found.

What is the intended message of singling out the pastor for specific rewards or acknowledgements? Is it because we believe the pastor is the most prominent member of the church body? Is it because we believe the pastor has sacrificed more than any other member of the church body? Is it because we believe that the hardship of pastoral ministry makes the pastor the most pitied member of the church body? Of course, none of these is true.

Maybe a Church Custodian Day would be a better idea. At least we can all agree that his job is as important as it is inglorious.

Regardless of the intended message of a pastor's reserved parking, I know what message my heart wants to receive: I deserve this. "I deserve this" is one of the deadliest sins of the shepherding ministry. It is the opposite of cross-bearing. It is the ministry of crown-wearing. Very quickly my heart believes that I am owed these special privileges that are afforded just one member of our church, me. I believe that I am entitled to these perks and if they are insufficiently provided, a debt is accumulated.

Of course, none of this is intended by these honoring gestures. But the average churchgoer has no idea just how corruptible my heart really is. My church members are too kind to believe that I am deeply tempted to settle for the lesser reward of flattery and public notice in place of the eternal reward of God's good favor.[1] What they don't realize is that pastor-leaders are probably even more susceptible to this than the average Joe. The pain of cross-bearing greatly strengthens my unhealthy appetite for flattery.

The Pharisees of Jesus's day operated from a religiously sanctioned ravenous appetite for flattery and recognition. The desire to be noticed and elevated was so powerful, Jesus offered a pretty extreme counter strategy. He knew it was not sufficient to go along

---

1. Matt 6:1: "Take care not to practice your righteousness in the sight of people, to be noticed by them; otherwise you have no reward with your Father who is in heaven."

with the public displays of acknowledgement while fighting the private temptation to grow overly dependent. So, he commanded us to get away. Don't go along. Get away. When you pray, when you fast, when you give, get away.[2] Run and hide. Your heart won't withstand the pressure to grasp at those delectable treats of self-esteem. So, change the game.

It is not sufficient for you to resist a growing sense of entitlement and deepening attachment to public recognition. You must counteract it by sometimes refusing those things that create the temptation.

Maybe start by parking in the back lot. The furthest spot away from the most convenient spot on your property. And every time you park there, remind yourself it is because you are the lowliest of servants. There is no shame in taking the worst parking spot. Do it for the joy set before you.

I will not settle for perks now. I am too fallible. I have invested all of my assets into my account of eternal rewards and I will not be robbed of that treasure for the trifling pleasantries of the here and now. The more I sacrifice now, the larger my account grows! The more I invest, the exponentially more I will receive. The more I give, the more indebted I become to my God and Savior, Jesus the firstborn, through whom my inheritance is secure. Do not weep for me!

Flee temptation. Decline a perk and see what your heart does. If it hurts to do so, you made the right choice. Humble yourself and he will lift you up.[3]

2. Matt 6:1–8.

3. 1 Pet 5:6: "Therefore humble yourselves under the mighty hand of God, so that He may exalt you at the proper time."

Chapter 26

JUMP

REFUSING TO PUT YOUR CHURCH TO THE TEST

When Satan says "jump" it's probably fair to question his intentions. When Satan tells a Son to jump into his Father's arms, an action otherwise benign and heartwarming takes on a sinister tone. Why would the Father of Lies who comes to steal, kill, and destroy, ask a Son to leap into his Father's embrace?

In this particular narrative, we are not left to wonder. It is a test. It is not a request to jump as an expression of the Son's desire for loving embrace. It is a request meant to establish a test of the Father's love.[1] The parameters of the test are specific but not established by the Father. And Satan took it to the extreme. He wasn't asking Jesus to find out how much the Father loved him, but whether the Father loved him at all. This was not a scaled rating, it was a pass/fail test—all or nothing. And Jesus refused.

A test is a measurement. Some tests measure what they claim to measure. Some tests do not. Some tests are valid, and some are not. If we were to construct a test of God's love, a proof of its existence or measurement of its quality, should not the Father weigh in on the validity of that test?

When my child asserts "If you love me, you will let me do this thing" I have every right to challenge the validity of my child's

---

1. Matt 4:5–7.

standard of measurement. What a child gauges as loving may be quite the opposite.

For this reason, the Scriptures prohibit tests of our own design. "Do not put God to the test." Jesus refused to instigate a test of his own design or of Satan's design. Because God will fail that test. God will always fail invalid tests of the quality and character of his love for us.

The omnipotent, omniscient God of the universe has committed to love us according to his good purposes, not ours. He loves us according to his definition of love, not ours, according to truth, not conjecture.

Extending this principle, I would suggest that people may fail the tests that God has already committed to fail, the tests I design. And yet as a shepherd leader I am constantly tempted both to construct these invalid tests and then to believe the invalid findings. These invalid tests with invalid findings become a source of pain in the life of the shepherd.

A pastor falls ill and misses ten full days of ministry, including two Sundays. This is the first time this pastor has ever had to deal with such a debilitating and prolonged sickness. Adding to the pain of his illness is the disappointment he feels related to the small number of people who bothered to check in. Without meaning to, he creates a test in his mind; if my church loved me, more of them would have checked in.

A leader has been more than willing to accept a small salary for many years in order to serve her church faithfully and consistently. She does not want to be a financial burden and is motivated by self-sacrificing love for her spiritual family. Her vehicle suffers an unrecoverable breakdown and she does not have the money to replace it. A week later, no one has asked her if she needs financial help. And without meaning to, she creates a test in her mind; if my church loved me, they would have asked me about my car.

A youth pastor is invited to discuss an "issue" with an elder of his church. During the meeting he discovers that a parent has brought a complaint about his leadership to this elder. As the complaint is discussed it becomes apparent that this elder did not defend the youth pastor when the issue was raised with the parent. The youth pastor is sick to his stomach at the realization that he's been hung out to dry. And without meaning to, he creates a test in his mind; if this elder loved me, he would have defended me against this parent's complaint.

The hidden, unacknowledged reality of these three wounding scenarios is that God failed the test before people did. God could have sent people to check in on this sick pastor, but he did not. God could have provided the money for a new car, but he did not. God could have moved in this elder's heart to defend the youth pastor, but he did not. Or at least not convincingly enough. Before people fail the test, God fails the test.

God does not love according to our understanding of love, but according to his. God's love is shown to us in this way, a cross.

There is no need to deny the pain of it. Gethsemane tells us it is permissible to wish for and pray for a plan B. Yes, it hurts to feel unloved. But just as you should never put God to the test, your people should not be subjected to those same tests. They will fail most of the time. If you jump from the temple, you will end up injured, on the ground, having plummeted from a great height.

When you learn to receive love from God as God expresses it, your cup will never run dry. You will cease putting the love of others to the test because you won't need such tests to know you are loved. God's love is perfect, it is unending, and it is *occasionally* glimpsed through the imperfect vessels of your brothers and sisters in Christ.

To catch a glimpse here and now is a gift.

Chapter 27

NEEDINESS

REFUSING TO BECOME A RESOURCE-CONSUMING CHURCH

As we sat with the missionary church planter and listened to the riddle of his situation, I was impressed by his calm ingenuity. I was with a team of teens I had brought to the Philippines, my home for many of my growing up years. We traveled to the outskirts of Manila and toured a handmade paper factory. At the end of our tour, we sat for a cold beverage and our tour guide explained the history and purpose of this humble enterprise.

He was sent to the Philippines to plant churches with the understanding that at a certain size, each church would begin financially supporting a local pastor. But the model didn't work. "The problem with our model is that even if you have a church of 200 and everyone is willing to give 10 percent, 10 percent of nothing is still nothing." These churches were growing in severely impoverished neighborhoods.

To solve this dilemma, the missionary started a handmade paper factory and employed each of the newly minted pastors as craftsman. Each of the workers I met that day was shepherding a congregation of his own. After putting in their hours mashing, spreading, and drying colored pulp, they would get to work caring for their flock.

My situation as a pastor looks a little different. If my town is anything like your town, maybe you can relate. Everyone is always fundraising. Schools are fundraising, sports clubs are fundraising, fine art groups are fundraising, aid organizations are fundraising, political groups are fundraising, para-church organizations are fundraising, and now individuals are fundraising through platforms like GoFundMe. We believe that money is the answer to many of our problems and there is nothing that convinces us more soundly than being a part of a culture and people awash in money.

God doesn't need money to advance his kingdom. A lack of money is not what stands in the way of you and your church fulfilling your kingdom calling. If you speak and act as if money is the pathway to greater impact in ministry, you are preaching a lie. You are preaching a lie that is believable only to the extent that we worship money.

We see gross examples of gargantuan money gobbling ministries and their wealthy leaders paraded on screen every day. They will stand before the judgement seat as you and I will. But in the meantime, I am tempted to find consolation by telling myself I am not like them. This reassurance misses the point.

The way my church talks about and prioritizes money is not just about standing before the judgment seat of God. The way my church talks about and prioritizes money is about being a contributing member of our community. It is about our testimony to our neighbors, our fellow Christian churches, our local nonprofits.

As a cross-bearing shepherd, I have already accepted that the first step in following Jesus is self-denial. And I cannot preach individual self-denial against the backdrop of organizational self-gratification. If a person in my church approached me and said "I am looking to give $10,000 to help someone in need and I wanted to give it to your family" I would direct the money to be given to someone else. My family is not "in need" by any standard measure. But if that same person approached me and said "I am looking to give $10,000 to meet local needs and I wanted to give it to your church" would I under any circumstances suggest giving the money elsewhere?

You may be tempted to believe that your small church budget is a cross that you have been called to bear. But if you sat for a few minutes with the paper-maker pastors in the slums of Manila, your self-pity would quickly evaporate. My desire for a larger ministry budget is influenced in part by my own pride and fears. I want to be successful according to the visible metrics that money provides and I lack sufficient faith in the God who promises to give me everything I need.

As discussed in prior chapters, I have a duty to watch over my heart with all diligence. Money will not make my ministry, but it can corrupt it. It corrupts the hearts of leaders who crave it and the public testimony of churches that ravenously consume it. Self-restraint is necessary. Deny yourself. If I never redirect money to other recipients, I am attached to money. Furthermore, if I cannot *happily* redirect money to some other recipient, I am attached to money. Try it: "If you want to help local families in need, maybe you should consider donating that money to the local food bank." And see how your heart feels after.

My inner voice tells me that the best use of the funds would be the local food bank but also tells me that if we accept the money and direct it through our church, we can get some credit for that generosity. This is my human nature at its worst. This is not secret generosity; this is pharisaical recognition purchasing. And God doesn't like it.

The decision to accept or redirect money is just like every other cross-bearing decision; I must be able hear from the Lord. Jesus knows where that money would be best used so ask him. He will lead you. And if you let him lead you, you will be blessed and others will be blessed through you.

EXAMEN

Chapter 28

IMPATIENCE

THE UNIQUENESS OF THE SHEPHERDING GIFT

Paul wasn't having it. He had tried and tried to reach his own people and was met with overwhelming opposition. He had been a Jewish man's man, a guy with power, influence, money, and a license to kill. And he had forfeited everything to follow Jesus. What could be more compelling?! His testimony was bulletproof! Surely his Jewish brothers would recognize he was telling the truth and see the light.

But they didn't. They pushed back. And Paul eventually reached his breaking point. He couldn't handle it, couldn't take it, couldn't see a way through it. So, he left. He shook the dust off his feet and got out of Dodge. "Since you repudiate it and judge yourselves unworthy of eternal life, behold, we are turning to the Gentiles."[1]

This turn of events launched Paul into the most famous missionary effort of all time. He would travel the world in dramatic fashion, find adventure, adversity, and victories in many foreign places. His faithful efforts have spawned missionary endeavors for two thousand years!

Paul is a hero.

But Peter stayed in Jerusalem.

---

1. Acts 13:46.

Peter has a different energy than Paul. Peter was called to remain in the area of Jerusalem and shepherd the young church there. He traveled a bit, to the surrounding areas, sometimes by direct invitation. But Peter knew that Peter was called to stay local and lead the church of his own people.

When Peter and Paul met up fourteen years after Paul's conversion, they acknowledged their different callings, and blessed each other.[2] Paul would travel the world and preach the good news to gentile communities spread over Asia and into Europe, and Peter would stay home and work it out with the locals. Peter had a grace and calling for the locals that Paul did not.

Cross-bearing shepherding ministry requires a particular grace to absorb the wounds of a specific crowd. Peter had a particular grace for the Jewish people with their unique cultural identity. He could see past the issues and envision God's redemptive work. Paul did not have that particular grace for those same people, so instead of bearing a cross for the Jews, he was led to find a different cross to bear. Paul wasn't less willing to suffer,[3] he was unwilling to suffer for *these* people. It wasn't his calling.

It is profoundly problematic to a local church when a Paul type decides to stick around and do Peter's job. The Paul type always talks about wanting to shake the dust of this place from his feet. But he stays. He may stay for any of a hundred reasons but he is clearly frustrated in his role. There were many factors impacting the ministry decisions of both Peter and Paul. I don't want to oversimplify their motives. And yet both were endowed with a certain gifting and grace that suited them for a unique calling. The same grace that suited each man for his calling, made him less suitable for an alternate calling.

Outside observers will be quick to note the fervor of the evangelistic/prophetic type. He speaks and preaches with a very high degree of conviction and is able to draw stark moral lines with authority. No one is debating his giftedness. But no one is really sure

2. Gal 2:1–9.
3. 2 Cor 11:23–27.

if he loves his shepherding role. His exasperation with his flock's pace of maturation may begin to bleed through his teaching.

He is a cross-bearer. And no one doubts just how heavy his cross really is, because they are reminded. People learn to accept that they are a stiff-necked bunch.

Poor pastor. He has to put up with our foolishness, our stubbornness.

In extreme cases, members of the flock learn to accept that tolerating their discontented pastor is their cross to bear. It doesn't feel very life-giving but they must not complain. He is clearly called. He is so godly. They must be the problem.

Some are called as apostles, some as evangelists, some prophets, and some as pastors and teachers.[4] If you are the apostle type, good at launching faith communities, Amen! We need you. If you are an evangelist, good at convincing the lost of their need for God, Amen! We need you. If you are a prophet, good at conveying God's heart on current matters in stark terms, Amen! We need you. Just don't become a lead pastor.

Shepherding is much like parenting. It is a long game. It is costly in every way that raising kids is costly. And if you are the kind of shepherd leader who cannot escape the mental fantasies of shaking the dust of this place from your feet, I give you permission to go. Ever met someone raised by parents who constantly expressed unhappiness in their role and duties as parents? That is what you are doing to your church. But you are different from parents in this respect; you can leave. You don't have to self-actualize your unhappiness with your role by emotionally flagellating your congregation.

It is my observation that our nation's church culture seems to have stoked this attitude most powerfully in evangelist leaders. If you went to Christian school, Bible college, Christian university, or seminary prior to the year 2000, it is very likely you took a class on personal evangelism. It is less likely you took a course on personal pastoring, personal prophecy, personal apostleship, personal administration, or personal helps. If you are gifted in evangelism,

4. Eph 4:11–13.

you probably left that course pumped up to an eleven. If you are like me and evangelism isn't your strength, you may have left wondering why you were so pathetic.

One distinguishing mark of an evangelist is that he or she does not have a cross-bearing grace for the slow and tedious work of shepherding ministry. And when the lead shepherd of a congregation does not have a special grace for pastoral ministry, the flock quickly learn to bear the cross of his incompatibility to the role.

The second mark of an evangelist is that nearly every sermon and teaching somehow becomes a salvation message. The goal is to get the unsaved saved. And the church needs to present this message and receive this message! But getting people saved isn't shepherding any more than giving birth is parenting. This congregation has grown to accept the cross-bearing ministry of starvation. Their leader is incapable of consistently offering the solid food needed for healthy growth across the maturation spectrum.

The church needs evangelists. Just not in the place of shepherds. This isn't a matter of being more or less gifted. This is a matter of which gift you have. Paul accepted his impatience as an indication of God's leading and his own calling. So, he left. Peter stayed. Evangelists are tasked with bringing the unbelieving into the flock. Shepherds care for the health of the flock to ensure that it remains a place where new believers are welcomed, grow and thrive.

Being a misfit to your ministry assignment will feel like a cross, but maybe it is one you should not continue to bear.

Chapter 29

SOUR WINE

FINDING TRUE REST FOR YOUR WEARY SOUL

I have reached the limits of my physical capacity only a few times in the last several years. Every time it has been on a hunting trip. Our Alaskan lifestyle affords many hunting opportunities and my family harvests moose and black bear every year. The meat that fills our freezer is enough to last until next year's hunting season. I enjoy being able to eat from the land in a sustainable way.

It is on these trips that I have been pushed to my absolute physical limit. Hiking for hours, packing loads that my legs can hardly bear, sometimes running out of food and water. Some moments all I could do was focus on taking the next step. Other moments I thought my heart might explode out of my chest. On a few occasions, I have even wondered if I would survive to tell the tale.

But I keep going back. Our hunting excursions account for only about two weeks of the year. There is something that happens during the fifty weeks in between. I tend to forget the pain, the extreme exhaustion and physical overload. All I remember is the adventure, the amazing scenery, finding success and an abundant reward!

This equation appears to be reversed for many shepherds: Fifty weeks of pushing the limits in the trenches followed by two weeks of respite and recovery. Except as shepherds, the exhaustion is much deeper. Mental and emotional fatigue take a significant toll, the recovery time is longer, and the process of recovery is more complex. I don't think it is an overstatement to say the majority of pastors and ministry leaders I have met over the years report a deep and unshakeable sense of being "tired."

In my own experience, rest has been something of a riddle. I would often point to external realities and limitations for my inability to really rest. The consequence of my inability to rest was an ever-diminishing net energy quotient. I was a little more tired this year than I was last year, had a little less energy this month than I had last month. I began to sense it was unsustainable.

Because I was not able to solve for my need of rest, I was substituting relief for rest. To find relief from the stress and secondhand trauma of ministry, I would find ways to distract myself. Certain activities trick my brain into temporarily forgetting about all the things that weigh me down. Fishing for salmon or halibut is a fantastic distraction. But fishing is only available to me at certain times of the year. Other times I find other distractions. Entertainment and social media provide a great way to distract my mind from the difficult things I am dealing with as a shepherd. For a few brief moments, I could be free. I didn't see the hidden danger in this.

After he was abused by the Pharisees and flogged by the Roman cohort, Jesus was forced to haul his heavy death instrument to its final resting place, Golgotha. Once there, the pain was not over. Jesus was to have his hands and feet nailed to the beam so that he could be lifted up and hung by his extremities. But before pounding in the nails, seemingly as an acknowledgment of his great agony, the Roman executioners offered Jesus sour wine with myrrh.[1] It was an anesthetic intended to provide him some reprieve from the pain, an escape. Jesus declined.

What I did not understand was that my method of escaping the weightiness and pain served to disconnect myself from myself. I was getting relief by closing myself off, by shutting down my own experience of myself. But when I disconnect from myself I

1. Matt 27:34.

unavoidably disconnect from God. When I disconnect from God I do not heal and therefore I do not rest.

I would often come to the end of my day of rest feeling no better off, sometimes even worse. I found no rejuvenation in "checking out" for a few hours. I was repeatedly doing what Jesus would not do, taking an anesthetic to numb myself. My form of anesthetic did not begin with a moral wrong but eventually ended that way. Distractions become snares become idols. My soul was not resting because I was looking for that rest somewhere other than through Jesus. To find my rest in Jesus requires me to be fully alive to the present moment with all of its pain and heartache so that I can fully experience him.

The truth is, I avoid myself because of the pain that I carry. To cease activity and to set aside distractions is to come face to face with me. This can feel like an emotional well too deep to plumb. I prefer to shut myself off to the hurt that others have caused and the shame I carry due to my own persistent failures. It's just too much. It has proven easier to hide away, to not feel. But to reiterate, to numb myself to pain is to numb myself to God.

So why am I so hesitant to face the pain if it is already there? It is not as though I have never faced hardship before. I face hard things all the time!

I think the reason I am so slow to acknowledge the stress, the exhaustion, the slights, and the wounds is because it all speaks of my vulnerability. I am not as capable, as indefatigable, as strong as I want to be, as I should have been. I am more easily wounded than I will ever admit. To face my pain is to face my frailty. So I exert a lot of energy convincing myself I am okay. That is what the job description calls for.

Much of this internal process happens beneath the level of my conscious awareness. I don't realize I am doing it. I'm so familiar with these tendencies, they are automatic. But as I began to explore my lack of rest, God started to reveal my heart. And then he extended this beautiful invitation:

"Come to Me, all who are weary and burdened, and I will give you rest. Take My yoke upon you and learn from Me, for I am gentle and humble in heart, and you will find rest for your souls. For My yoke is easy, and My burden is light."[2]

The invitation is to those who are exhausted, those who feel the load is too heavy. The promise is rest for your soul. And the instruction is to come to Jesus. Jesus is our only true rest. We find it in him when we come to him in our weariness and with all of our burdens. He doesn't offer a pep talk, a better strategy to get more done, an encouragement to suck it up. He offers rest and a lighter load. A mentor once told me "If you are carrying a load that is too heavy, it is either a load God does not intend you to carry or you are carrying it in a manner God does not intend."

To experience the rest only Jesus provides is to prolong my ministry as a cross-bearing shepherd. To rest is to set aside my utility and just be. True rest is not self-serving, it is the self-sacrifice of ceasing all striving, presenting myself to Jesus, sitting at his feet, and receiving from him. It is here that he sustains me, encourages me, heals me and strengthens me for another day.

I no longer avoid my weakness. I no longer numb my pain. I refuse the sour wine. And if I am so exhausted all I can think about is my very next step, it is one step toward him. He is the joy set before me.

2. Matt 11:28–30.

Chapter 30

THE MOST IMPORTANT THING
A FINAL WORD ABOUT FINAL WORDS

So how do you know you got it right? How do you know your heart has been truly transformed into the heart of a self-sacrificing leader, a shepherding cross-bearer? There is one final test of the quality of your alignment with the mission and model of Jesus: leaving.

The risk of damage to my ministry and my own reputation seems never more acute than in the final hours of my service. It is in the midst of departure that shepherds harm their flocks and undermine their own legacies. The painful memory of many wounds, many slights, many ingratitudes, come flooding into the leader's heart and mind with unexpected force. And the leader's imminent departure weakens the filters that have long been held firmly in place. There is nothing to lose now. Or so it seems.

Some leaders act out in grotesque ways, like using a final Sunday to spew pent-up anger from the preacher's pulpit. Others handle this emotional turmoil in passive-aggressive ways like subtly communicating to church leaders that farewell festivities and pleasantries are insufficiently grand. And yet others just shut down emotionally, avoiding goodbyes and final moments by hiding from the flock over the final days.

Saying goodbye has a way of revealing the truth of our cross-bearing. It is in saying goodbye that my subconscious motivations coming charging into the foreground. It is in saying goodbye that my worst transactional tendencies surface. Over my years of service, in some small way, I was buying gratitude, recognition, and respect. For some it is nothing more noble than flattery and pity. But the sacrifices of ministry will never be economically offset by these rewards. It always ends up being too steep a price. To the extent that I was purchasing these temporal rewards for my self-esteem, I realize I was ripped off.

The weight of what I have forfeited for these people is never felt more heavily than in the final moments before parting ways. I gave everything. I laid down my life. I forfeited weekends. I lost sleep. I lived on a modest income. I absorbed insults. I laid down my rights when others wouldn't. I put it all on the line for the ministry. And in these final moments I discover the depth of my resentment over how little I was given in return.

Only cross-bearing will save me from this. Cross-bearing ministry is a gift to God, an investment into eternity for which I will receive an incomprehensibly great reward. A cross-bearing shepherd ends each day by entrusting the result of my many sacrifices to the only one who can be trusted with such valuable payments. My service was to follow the one who showed me the way. My joy was to find that he was the way.

The more the cross-bearer gives, the greater the reward extends—far beyond what I deserve. His payments are grossly and excessively generous given my feeble ability. So great is his remuneration plan, I find myself only further in his debt as I give him my all. As I increase my sacrifice, he increases my reward more than a hundredfold.[1] As I enlarge my gift, I only experience more of him.

---

1. Mark 10:29–30: "Jesus said, 'Truly I say to you, there is no one who has left house or brothers or sisters or mother or father or children or farms, for My sake and for the gospel's sake, but that he will receive a hundred times as much now in the present age, houses and brothers and sisters and mothers and children and farms, along with persecutions; and in the age to come, eternal life.'"

And here is the tragic truth: Jesus made this clear; to the extent that I have served lesser rewards, those will be my *only* reward. To the extent that I served my own need for respect, that will be my only reward. To the extent that I served the building-up of my own self-esteem, that will be my only reward. To the degree that I sought the flattery of others, that will be my only reward. How sad. How pathetic. And I must painfully admit, how familiar.

It is the emptiness, the hollowness of these lesser rewards that nurtures my own feelings of victimization and resentment. I served the meeting of my own basic needs and yet these needs were so poorly met. I needed significance and acknowledgment but honestly, I didn't get a very good deal. I paid a heavy price for a lousy reward. These disappointed shepherds, when the dam of stockpiled dissatisfaction finally breaks, give into anger and woundedness. Some let it spew, some let it seep out, and others don't know what to do with it but hide.

Congregations will surely forgive a pastor for a bad moment. After ten years of service, who wouldn't forgive a bad final ten days? The bigger issue is that these final moments reveal the shepherd's heart and the shepherd's ambitions. People intuitively sense that this angst isn't new, it just finally showed through. And in this moment, they are left to conclude two things; this pastor was never happy and we were a bad flock.

Paul is clear; build on anything other than Christ, and the reward for your labor will be lost.[2] He didn't mean talk about Christ. He didn't mean preach accurate doctrine about Christ. He sternly warned, if your ambition is anything other than Christ, your ministry is a sham.

So today, right now, before you lay your head to rest on your pillow, give all the slights, the wounds, the insults, the ingratitude to Jesus. Entrust it all to him. Forgive and hold no one in your debt. Jesus, this is all for you.

---

2. 1 Cor 3:12–13: "Now if anyone builds on the foundation with gold, silver, precious stones, wood, hay, or straw, each one's work will become evident; for the day will show it because it is to be revealed with fire, and the fire itself will test the quality of each one's work."

Do not pity me. I take up my cross for the joy set before.

And when you arrive at your last day, this healing truth will wash over your grieving soul;

My journey of cross-bearing benefitted no one more than me.

ADDENDUMS

Chapter 31

NEPOTISM

REGARDING FAMILY RELATIONSHIPS

I recently listened to a frustrated employee describe his employers' decision to give company leadership to their son. This man was annoyed because he felt the son did not deserve the role. He end-capped his irritated explanation with "Nepotism sucks." I understand his frustration. But I am not sure he understands the nature of nepotism.

It is not nepotism to give what you own to your children. That is called parenting. It is not nepotism when I put dinner on the table for my children but not for yours. I provide and care for my own family as an assignment from God.

Nepotism is using a position of influence *inappropriately* to grant benefits to *undeserving* family members. If a pastor fills an open staff position with a family member it would qualify as nepotism for the following reasons; 1) The money used to hire the staff member is not the pastor's money, 2) the family member is not the most qualified candidate for the position, and 3) the pastor bypassed decision-making stakeholders in making the hire.

I pastor in a small community. Almost everyone is related to someone. As a result, nepotism is sometimes used as a subtle jab against our leadership credibility. Because I care about our leadership's credibility, my natural inclination would be to rule out family members for positions of influence in our church. But imagine having leadership gifting and discovering you are disqualified from ever serving at your church as a matter of your biological origin.

As a cross-bearing shepherd, I must not be seduced into managing public perception of me or my church. I must do what is in the best interest of the health of our church and each of its members.

I believe an honest and healthy approach is to 1) ensure that biological relationship doesn't wholly qualify or disqualify a person from serving in leadership, 2) listen to your leaders on these decisions and don't make the decision alone, and 3) avoid stacking your leadership teams with family members so you do not succumb to homogeneity and group think. Your church will be healthiest when leaders represent a diverse set of viewpoints.

With that said, you may also want to consider where you plan to spend Thanksgiving over the next several years. If you place family members in positions of authority, it is at least reasonable to assume that one day one of you may have to fire the other! If my relative is a church elder, that relative may have to make the hard decision to let me go. If my relative is an employed staff member, I may have to make the hard decision to let him or her go. If there is a church leadership catastrophe, it may be nice to have some family left that isn't directly involved.

At the time of this writing, I have extended family members that serve on our staff team, our board of directors, and as church elders. We have essentially set the limit at about two per group, although that is not an official limit. I have other family members that are highly qualified and yet do not serve in any of those official capacities because it would put us over the threshold of tolerability. Each of my family members that serve was appointed by a decision of the group with which they serve. I do not make those decisions alone.

We try our best to avoid actual nepotism while accepting some unearned perceptions of it.

Chapter 32

KIDS

REGARDING YOUNG PEOPLE GROWING UP

One of the great joys of shepherding in one place over many years is the opportunity to watch families form and grow. Kids turn into parents who have kids who become parents. It is an amazing miracle to behold. And I get to offer spiritual guidance and encouragement as these families grow. It is a privilege.

Over years of observation, I have found that there are essentially three kinds of kids you will see grow up in your church. There are the struggling kids, the nominal kids, and the involved kids. *Struggling kids* are the ones who develop an early reputation for bad decisions and unhealthy lifestyles. The family is part of your church, but the kid doesn't like it. *Nominal kids* come from nominal families who have no strong feelings about church and exhibit no strong commitments. They are easy to have around but rarely engage. *Involved kids* are the ones who show up to everything and want to help with everything. Church provides these kids a sense of purpose and community and they eat it up.

My small-town church faces two kid-related challenges: 1) letting struggling kids move beyond the reputations of their youth, and 2) placing developmentally appropriate boundaries around involved kids. Self-serving leaders will shun struggling kids while using up involved kids. Cross-bearers must approach youth differently.

If we don't provide redemptive pathways for struggling youth to move beyond their reckless youthfulness within the confines of their faith community, they will have no choice but to grow somewhere else. Talk to any person who lived within the same small community through adolescence into adulthood and they will tell you, "It's hard to move past the reputation of my youth." Even well-meaning people will joke about your past in a way that suggests it still defines you—in a way that makes you feel like a child.

Redemptive cross-bearing requires me to give people a chance to change their ways, even if I might regret it. Opportunities for involvement should be consistent with the person's current maturity level but should communicate "We believe you can be better, and we want to partner with Jesus to get you there." When prodigals are embraced by their faith family, real transformation is possible.

The trickier issue for me is the need for boundaries around involved kids. A thirteen-year-old who was born into your ministry wants to help with nursery every single Sunday for the rest of her life. And to be honest, she is a great helper and we can always use great helpers. But she is motivated in part because she doesn't want to sit through the Sunday service. Hanging out with babies and small children is more enjoyable. Serving is an important part of her growth in God but so is integration into the corporate worship and teaching ministry.

Involved kids can easily get sucked up into the engine of church programs in a way that stunts overall development. And churches that function from a position of neediness will readily accept this free assistance. But taking more than you are giving is the opposite of cross-bearing. Using up involved kids without nurturing them reveals a consumer mindset. This will eventually corrupt these kids' view of the church and of themselves.

Some young people are gifted enough to find opportunities in ministry with little oversight. A young musician discovers that she can sing on any worship team she wants, so she looks for the one that demands the least while granting the most creative freedom. Leaders say "We trust you" while unwittingly creating space for the cultivation of the teen's narcissism. A cross-bearing shepherd refuses to use people at the expense of developing people.

It doesn't matter how badly I feel I need the help. When programs take precedence over people, people are worn out in service of programs. When people take precedence over programs, people grow and some programs necessarily die. If I am willing to sacrifice short-term gains for long-term growth, the kids in my church are more likely to grow up loving and serving the church.

I will readily admit that this is a difficult challenge. But there are a few guidelines we have implemented along the way to maintain an investment posture with our young people: 1) volunteers must attend a majority of our Sunday services. If their ministry involvement keeps them out of church, they can volunteer once a month or two out of every six weeks. 2) Young volunteers have a direct supervisor who will include them in the same equipping/ encouragement opportunities as the adult volunteers. 3) Youth cannot serve a portion of a meeting and then skip out on the rest of it. For example, a teen cannot serve on the worship team and then skip the teaching and discussion portion of our youth meetings.

Kids might tell you it is fine. Parents might tell you it is fine. But allowing kids to serve without boundaries is not fine. First serve them. Let them learn from your example of self-sacrificing, cross-bearing love and they will thrive.

Chapter 33

FOOD

REGARDING YOUR PHYSICAL HEALTH

I didn't really start putting on weight until I was in my thirties. I was skinny as a high school student and could put away a nearly unlimited number of calories. While working in construction as a teenager, I would often down a McDonald's supersize double quarter pounder with cheese meal with an extra double quarter pounder with cheese and two refills of my supersized coke. This usually took less than ten minutes. I am no longer proud of this as I once was.

Then something happened. I stopped burning all the calories I was eating. I remember the first time I saw a picture of myself and thought "I am putting on more weight than I realized." This happened in part because I was in pastoral ministry. And because I was drinking vanilla breves with whipped cream. Working while sitting and sipping straight half-and-half did not serve me well.

There are many reasons a person might want to lose weight. Most of them have to do with looking good. I want to look good. But this isn't a sufficient motivation for most people to stay in shape. For a shepherd, such a motivation may not serve well. It is an awkward dichotomy when a spiritual shepherd is driven by a concern for outward appearances.

But there is a good motivation for keeping healthy. Crosses are heavy and will require all your energy. Healthy social, emotional, and mental habits and lifestyles are supported by a healthy body. A good diet and exercise provide the needed physical resources to accomplish everything that God has called you to do. Bad diet and lack of exercise make a shepherd lethargic, uninspired, and distracted.

Honest confession: I still enjoy unhealthy foods and sedentary activities. It was easy for me to blame stress as the source of my lethargy and lack of inspiration. But cross-bearing requires me to forfeit some things for the sake of eternity. So, I skip it. Not my will but yours be done.